SECESSION
CONSIDERED AS A RIGHT IN THE STATES COMPOSING THE LATE AMERICAN UNION AND JUSTIFICATION OF THE SOUTHERN STATES IN EXERCISING THE RIGHT

by
Alexander H. Handy
"A Gentleman of Mississippi"

THE CONFEDERATE
REPRINT COMPANY
☆ ☆ ☆ ☆
WWW.CONFEDERATEREPRINT.COM

Secession
by Alexander H. Handy

Originally Published in 1863
by South-West Confederate Printing House
Jackson, Mississippi

Reprint Edition © 2015
The Confederate Reprint Company
Post Office Box 2027
Toccoa, Georgia 30577
www.confederatereprint.com

Cover and Interior by
Magnolia Graphic Design
www.magnoliagraphicdesign.com

ISBN-13: 978-0692466827
ISBN-10: 0692466827

INTRODUCTION

To the patriot, who maintains the justice of the separation of the Confederate States from the United States, it is of vital importance to feel assured that the right of a State to secede from the Union with the United States, whenever she thought fit to exercise it, was perfect and absolute, beyond the power of denial or molestation from any source.

Upon this mainly depends the questions, what political relations subsist between the seceded States and the remaining United States; and whether the citizens of such States, in defending themselves by arms against the invasion of the United States, set on foot to enforce the laws of the United States over such States, after secession, are to be regarded as traitors and rebels, on the one hand, or as absolved from all political connection with the United States, and acting in the defense of their legitimate rights, on the other.

If the secession be without right, the position of the people of a State resisting the authority of the

United States is that of *rebellion* against legitimate power, and the armed resistants are traitors and felons; but if it be rightful and in the exercise of the legitimate powers of the State, then, the attempt at coercion by invasion and making war against the State is a usurpation and an outrage which the State is bound to repel as an attempt to destroy her rights and liberties by mere brute force. It is, therefore, a question which must most seriously impress every true patriot and every elevated mind in the South – had the State *the right* to secede in her sovereign capacity, for reasons which she judged sufficient to demand and justify her secession?

If this enquiry be resolved in the affirmative, it becomes important to consider, whether the circumstances, under which the State thought fit to exercise the right, are such as to justify her, in the estimation of mankind, in the exercise of it.

These two questions will, therefore, form the subject for consideration in these remarks; first, whether one of the States constituting the United States had the right to secede from the Union; and, secondly, whether the circumstances under which the right was exercised by the Southern States justify its exercise and acquit those Southern States of any bad faith to the obligations of the Union.

ONE
☆ ☆ ☆ ☆

First – As to the abstract right of secession.

This right is claimed as resulting, from the rights and powers which the several States had when they formed the Constitution; and from the nature and purposes of the Union created by the Constitution, as shown by its face and by the history of its formation and adoption.

1. In the first place, each State was, at the time of the adoption of the Constitution, a sovereign and independent State, and acted as such in adopting the Constitution. This is manifest – from the Declaration of Independence, which proclaims the several States to be "free and independent States" – from the second of the Articles of Confederation of 1778, which declares that "each State retains *its sovereignty, freedom* and *independence,* and every power, jurisdiction and right, which is not thereby expressly delegated to the United States" – from the treaty of peace with Great Britain, after the close of the war of the revolution, recognising each State by name as

a "free, sovereign and independent State" – and finally, by the sanction of the Supreme Court of the United States, in the early history of the Union, in the case of *Ware vs. Hylton*, 3d Dallas' Rep., 199, in which it is held by Judge Chase, that the effect of the Declaration of Independence was "not that the united colonies *jointly,* in a *collective* capacity, were independent States, but that *each State of them was a sovereign and independent State"* – a doctrine recognised by numerous subsequent decisions of that Court.

It is also incontrovertibly true, that each State for herself, in her sovereign political capacity, by her Legislature, and not by immediate election of the people, appointed delegates to the Convention which formed the Constitution – that the votes given in the Convention, in its formation, were given by States and not *per capita;* each State being entitled to but one vote upon every question, regardless of the relative number of delegates – and finally, each State, for herself, and in her sovereign capacity, accepted, ratified and *acceded to* the Constitution; and it was of no force or effect upon her, until so ratified and acceded to by her, she remaining, meanwhile, a separate sovereign State, to all intents and purposes.

Notwithstanding these conclusive facts, incontestibly establishing that each State was a separate sovereign State, before the adoption of the Constitution, President Lincoln, in his message of July, 1861, boldly declares that "no one of them was ever a State out of the Union," that "the word *sovereignty* is not in the national Constitution, nor, as is believed, in any of the State Constitutions" – that "the Union is older than any of the States, and, in act, it created them as States." This last is said with reference to the Union under the Articles of Confederation; which he considers in some way blended with the Union under the present Constitution. But the Union under the Articles of Confederation was entirely abrogated upon the adoption of the Constitution by the States; each State acceded to the Constitution in her sovereign political capacity, as is above shown, and thereby established a new and distinct Union; the States refusing to adopt it, remaining free and independent States, absolved from the old Union and totally disconnected with that formed under the present Constitution, until they acceded to the latter. Of course, the rights and powers of the States, as members of the Union, can only be affected by the Union created by the present Constitution.

Reckless and unfounded as are these asseverations, the position assumed by them will be found, after a careful examination of the subject, to be the only theory upon which the right of the States to interpose their sovereign power against the usurpations of the Federal Government can be successfully denied; and it must be considered, from the imposing authority and the solemn circumstances under which it is put forth, as having been taken advisedly, as the ground on which the government of the United States rests its right to wage a war of subjugation and extermination against the people of the Confederate

States for attempting to resume their original *status* of separate, sovereign States in all respects. Yet, it is so utterly unfounded in truth and in history, that no further answer to it is required than the reference to the historical facts above stated.

Each State, then, being sovereign when she ratified the Constitution, must have continued such after her ratification, except so far as she restricted herself of her sovereign powers by the Constitution; unless she absolutely surrendered her sovereignty. And here the vital question arises, did the States, in ratifying the Constitution, part with the sovereign right of judging, each for herself, whether the powers conferred on the Government by the Constitution, or the rights and powers retained by the States had been violated; and did the States bind themselves to an indissoluble Union?

2. If we consider *the purpose* for which the Constitution was formed, we find nothing that binds the States to a Union irrevocable under any circumstances.

These purposes are stated in the letter of the Convention – signed by Gen. Washington, accompanying the Constitution, and which was submitted to the Convention of the several States with the Constitution – to be, "that the power of making war, peace and treaties; that of levying money and regulating commerce, and the correspondent executive and judicial authorities shall be fully and effectually vested in the General Government of the Union." The object was merely to supply the defects existing under the Articles of Confederation, in these respects; to *entrust* the necessary powers, *in these particulars,* to a general head; because from their nature they could not be exercised either by the States separately, nor by the Union under the Articles of Confederation. This was done in the Constitution by creating a government to execute these powers, delegating them fully to it, prohibiting to the States all counteracting powers, and clothing the Government with all the power, legislative, executive and judicial, necessary to the complete exercise of the powers entrusted to it.

But these powers are all *"delegated,"* in express terms; which shows that the Federal Government was intended to be but the *agent* and *representative* of the States; and as stated by Mr. Madison, in *Federalist*, No. 45, *"the powers delegated to the Federal Government are few and defined. Those which are to remain to the State governments are numerous and indefinite.* The former will be exercised principally on external objects, as war, peace, negotiation and foreign commerce, with which last the power of taxation will, for the most part, be connected. *The powers reserved to the several States will extend to all the objects, which, in the ordinary course of affairs, concern the lives, liberty and properties of the people, and the internal order, improvement and prosperity of the State."* It was admitted freely by the advocates of the Constitution, that the great elements of strength and power remained in the States; insomuch that they feared that the States would prove to be too strong for the effective operation of the Federal Government, rather than that the latter would interfere with the powers of the States (See *Federalist*, Nos. 27, 31, 45); whilst the most wise and sagacious of its friends, considered that its true theory and glory were *strong States and a weak Federal head,* whose strength consisted in its members and not of itself, and was only such as was necessary to execute the few powers plainly delegated to it.

3. In its *nature* and *character,* the Constitution was a *compact* between the States, and the Union formed under it, was *Federal.* This is clear, from the following considerations:

1. It was formed by the States acting in their political capacities, and not by the aggregate mass of the people of all the States; and it was ratified and acceded to in the same manner by each State for herself; those not acceding to it being wholly free from its operation and remaining independent sovereign States.

2. It declares, in the 7th article, that the ratifications of the Conventions of nine States should be sufficient to establish it *"between the States"* so ratifying it – which clearly shows that *the States as such were the parties to it,* and that it was a compact *between* them as such.

3. Amendments to it are to be acted on by each State in her political capacity, by her Legislature, or by a convention appointed by her and under her own laws, each acting separately.

4. The powers not delegated are reserved to the States or to the people, by the 10th amendment – that is, to the States, so far as their exercise may be matter of political power; and to the people of each State, so far as the same may be matter of individual right, under the Constitution and laws of the State.

5. It was denominated a *Federal* Constitution by its advocates in recommending its ratification (see *Federalist passim*), the Union formed by it was called a *Confederate Republic* (*Federalist*, No. 9), and it was characterized, in the more essential and controlling points of the *foundation* and the *extent of its powers,* as Federal; while in the minor matter of *the execution of its granted powers only,* it was said to be national. (*Federalist*, No. 39). It was received in popular acceptation and called a Federal Constitution – an idea so universally received and so popular that it was assumed as the name of the great party which came into power upon the organization of the Government, and held it until that party proved to entertain principles and views subversive of the true spirit of the Constitution, and in the meantime laid the foundation of doctrines which have led to its prostration.

6. It was received and adopted by the States as a compact between each other. While this is manifest from the history of the ratifications of all the States in their conventions, it is expressly stated in the ratifications of Massachusetts and New Hampshire, and was, in a few years thereafter, also expressly declared by Virginia, Kentucky, and several

other States, in the memorable contest which arose upon the alien and sedition laws in 1798.

It was a compact between sovereign States for a union between them, for *certain specified purposes,* to promote the common defense and general welfare of its members. Its basis was that great principle of American institutions – *the consent of the parties to it;* and when that is withdrawn, and the parties refuse to comply with the terms necessary to continue its operation, its existence must cease, since there is no provision – and from the nature of the Union there could not be – for its continuance by coercion; but of this hereafter.

The doctrine is well established, that "several sovereign and independent States may unite themselves together by a perpetual confederacy, without each, in particular, ceasing to be an independent State. They will form together a Federal Republic: the deliberations in common will offer no violence to the sovereignty of each member, though they may, in certain respects, put some constraint on the exercise of it, in virtue of voluntary engagements" (Vattel, *Law of Nations*, book 1, chap. 1, sec. 10). And this is clearly the nature of the Union of the States, under the Constitution of the United States, whether it be called a Government, a confederacy, or a compact. *"The proposed Constitution,"* says Mr. Hamilton, *"so far from implying an abolition of the State Governments, makes them constituent parts of the national sovereignty"* (*Federalist*, No. 9). *"The State Governments may be regarded,"* says Mr. Madison, "*as constituent and essential parts of the Federal Government* (*ibid*, No. 45).

It is perfectly manifest that the Constitution did not merge the States in this Federal Union, and annihilate their political existence and powers. Unlike the articles of Union of the United Kingdom of Great Britain, the Union was *Federate* in its character, the States retaining their sovereign character and most essential powers; whereas, in that of England and Scotland, in the language of the learned commentator on the laws of England, "the two contracting States are totally annihilated, without any power of revival, and a third arises from the conjunction, in which all the rights of sovereignty, and particularly that of legislation, must reside." This author states the difference between the character of the former and the latter kind of Government – that in a union of the latter description, an infringement of its conditions would not justify a dissolution; while in the case of a union of the former character, an infringement would certainly rescind the compact (1 Blackstone's *Commentaries*, 98, in note).

In such a case, the sovereign character is preserved; and it must, of necessity, be capable of vindicating its rights, by a resumption of the delegated powers; for otherwise, its sovereignty would be nugatory – indeed it would be virtually annihilated; and it is perfectly evident from the entire history of the formation and ratifications of the Constitution, that it was the especial care of the States to preserve their sovereignty.

There is, therefore, nothing in the purposes for which the Constitution was formed, nor in its nature and character, to bind the States to a perpetual Union under it, under all circumstances; or to debar each of them of the high sovereign power of vindicating her rights by resuming her original powers entirely whenever she considered that the fundamental conditions of the Union had been broken by the Government, or were about to be perverted to her oppression.

It was this right which justified the States in abrogating the Union made by the Articles of Confederation in disregard of a positive stipulation that it should be perpetual; and in establishing the present Constitution of the United States in a different mode from that prescribed in the Articles, and therein positively declared to be the only mode in which they should be altered. This course could only be justified on the principle of the right of secession; and it was so justified. When it was objected by some of the States that the Constitution was adopted in violation of these solemn stipulations and prohibitions against the consent of several of the States, the course was defended by its advocates on the ground of "the great principle of self-preservation," and of "the transcendent law of nature and of nature's God, which declares that the safety and happiness of society are the objects at which all political institutions aim, and *to which all such institutions must be sacrificed*" (*Federalist*, No. 43). There was no question as to the *right of the majority* to take this step, and it could not be justified on that ground; because the rights of the minority were positively placed beyond the control or power of the majority by the prohibitions of the Articles of Confederation. The power to abolish that form of government was placed solely on the great right of American liberty to alter or abolish any form of government whenever the safety and happiness of society required it – a right never parted with and incapable of alienation – a principle as fully applicable to the Constitution of the United States as to the Union under the Articles of Confederation; and even more so, since in the former, the mode of alteration is merely authorized; whereas in the latter, it is prescribed and *all other modes of alteration are positively prohibited:* a principle which as fully justifies secession as practised by the Confederate States as it did the abrogation of the Articles of Confederation in violation of the solemnly plighted faith of the States made in the adoption of that form of Union, and against the consent of several of them. The right then exercised was secession – the resumption by the States of their inherent sovereign powers, in their own discretion and for their happiness.

  4. But this right does not stand alone upon the nature and character of the Union, nor upon the general reservation of rights and powers in the Constitution – clear and unquestionable as it is on these grounds. It was matter of *express and positive reservation* by several of the States in the ratifications of the Constitution, and was plainly intended to be re-

served by all.

New York, in her resolutions of ratification, declared:

"That the powers of government may be resumed by the people, whensoever it shall become necessary to their happiness: that every power, jurisdiction and right, which is not, by said Constitution, clearly delegated to the Congress of the United States, or the departments of the government thereof, remains *to the people of the several States,* or to *their respective State Governments"* (1 Elliott's *Debates,* 361).

Rhode Island, in her ratification, declared:

"That the powers of government may be resumed by the people whensoever it shall become necessary to their happiness" (ibid., 369).

Virginia declared, in her ratification:

"That the powers granted under the Constitution, being derived from the people of the United States, *may be resumed by them whensoever the same shall be perverted to their injury and oppression"* (ibid.).

That the language, "may be resumed *by the people,"* was intended to mean *the people of the States, as States,* is most manifest.

In the first place, the powers were delegated *by the States as such,* and could not be said to be "*resumed*" except by the same political body which granted them. They never resided in the people of the United States; and hence, upon the failure of the Union, the people of the United States could not be said to "resume" them; but resumption imports *retaking by the authority which originally possessed them* – that is, the States in their political capacity. In the second place, the ratifications of several other of the States, in stating the reservation of powers not delegated to the United States, reserve them to the States, omitting the addition, *"or to the people"* – which shows that these latter words contained in the Tenth Amendment, and the equivalent words, *"resumed by the people,"* meant *the people of the States severally;* and that the true intent of this amendment and of the reservations in the ratifications of the States, was to retain the undelegated powers to the people of the several States, as sovereign communities, *to be exercised by them under their constitutions and laws;* that is to say, in their sovereign capacities. This clearly appears from the ratifications of Massachusetts, New Hampshire, New York, Pennsylvania and South Carolina.

Massachusetts: "That it be explicitly declared that all powers not expressly delegated by the aforesaid Constitution, are reserved *to the several States, to be by them exercised.*"

New Hampshire: "That it be explicitly declared that all powers not expressly and particularly delegated by the aforesaid Constitution, are reserved *to the several States, to be by them exercised.*"

Pennsylvania: "All the rights of sovereignty, which are not by the said Constitution expressly and plainly vested in the Congress, shall be deemed to remain with, and shall be exercised *by the several*

States in the Union, according to their respective Constitutions."

New York has been quoted above.

South Carolina: "That no section or paragraph of the said Constitution warrants a construction that *the States* do not retain every power not expressly relinquished by them, and vested in the General Government of the Union."

It was these declarations which caused the engrafting of the Ninth and Tenth Amendments into the Constitution; and furnish the true and proper exposition to the words, "the people," in these amendments; showing them to mean the *people of the States respectively in their sovereign capacity.* And this is equally true of the same words used contemporaneously in the ratifications above mentioned.

And now, when challenged to adduce positive authority for the right of secession, and for the doctrine that the States did not intend to bind themselves by the Constitution, to an indissoluble union, under all circumstances, we point to these solemn declarations of the States in their ratifications of the Constitution, and to the Ninth and Tenth Amendments which were produced by these declarations, as clear and positive proof that *the Union was established upon the express condition that the States respectively had the right to resume their powers of sovereignty delegated by the Constitution,* whensoever they considered that their happiness and safety demanded it.

The right of judging of this matter must necessarily reside in each State; because the reservation of power is to the States *respectively;* and from its very nature, each State must decide for herself. It could not apply to the States in the aggregate, or to a majority of them; both because of its nature, and because it is not so reserved. Hence the right, to be of any value, and especially to be consistent with the principles on which the Union was founded, must appertain to each State respectively.

It is not necessary that this right should be specified in the Constitution. It was not the office of that instrument to enumerate the reserved rights of the States, and no government makes provision for its own dissolution. It is sufficient if the right existed when the Constitution was acceded to by the States, and was not clearly parted with in that instrument. And how does the question thus stand?

When the Union was formed, the principle set forth in the Declaration of Independence was recognised as a fundamental doctrine, in all its force and extent, by all the States, and cherished as the palladium of our liberty – that whenever *any form of government* becomes destructive of the ends for which it was established, IT IS THE RIGHT OF THE PEOPLE TO ALTER OR ABOLISH IT, AND TO INSTITUTE A NEW GOVERNMENT, laying its foundations on such principles, and organizing its powers in such form, as to them shall be most likely to effect their safety and happiness." It was upon this high principle that the States were declared "free and independent States," and came into being as sovereign

States. And the basic principle on which all republican governments rest, and especially those of these States, is, "that governments derive their just powers from the consent of the governed." Assuredly this inestimable right was never intended to be impaired in the formation and adoption of the Constitution of the United States. Nay, it is positively shown that it was upon this very principle, that the formation and adoption of this Constitution – which were in palpable violation of the Articles of Confederation – were justified by its advocates, as is above shown.

It was regarded as a high and sacred right, appertaining to the people of the States when the Constitution was formed; and not only was not parted with in that instrument, but it was positively reserved.

The Ninth Amendment declares, that "the enumeration in the Constitution of certain *rights,* shall not be construed to deny or disparage others retained by the people." This is a positive reservation of all *individual rights* appertaining to the people of the States, under their respective State governments, whether enumerated or not; and it was introduced from abundant caution, to exclude the possibility of the legal implication that other rights, not enumerated, were denied to the citizen or delegated to the Government.

Of the same character is the Tenth Amendment, "that the powers not delegated to the United States by the Constitution, nor prohibited by it to the States, are reserved to the States respectively or to the people;" that is to say, to the States, or *to the people of the States, respectively,* in *their sovereign political capacity as States,* to be exercised and enjoyed according to the Constitution and laws of each State; because it was in that capacity alone that the several States acted in forming and adopting the Constitution, and became parties to the compact. And it is manifest from the history of these amendments that their scope and object were to place beyond question and beyond the possibility of interference by the Federal Government the rights and powers of the people of the States, held and enjoyed under their respective State governments, and not delegated nor prohibited in the Constitution.

Thus all the rights and powers of each State and of her people under their respective State governments, not enumerated and not delegated nor prohibited, are expressly retained. The purpose of the Constitution was not to specify the rights retained, but to enumerate those delegated to the United States. Hence, if a right existed in a State at the formation of the Constitution, and be not enumerated among the "delegated powers," or "prohibited rights," in the Constitution, it remains to the States. It is thus that all the numerous rights and powers of civil administration in the several States, and the individual rights of the citizen under their respective State governments, not reserved by enumeration, nor prohibited in the Constitution, are retained by the respective States.

Now it is incumbent on those who claim that

this high power, this invaluable right, this distinguishing principle of American liberty, was given up by the sovereign States in the Constitution, to show clearly where and how that was done. It will not do to rest its surrender upon plausible refinements and doubtful theories; for it must be presumed that if this right, which was considered so sacred by the framers of the Constitution, and so inestimable by the States, had been intended to be parted with or impaired, it would have been done in language not to be mistaken. And, therefore, if the question be merely left in doubt, whether the right is surrendered, it is the part of wisdom and safety to resolve it in favor of the retention of the right; since in cases of doubt, it is always safest, according to principles of American government, to entrust high powers with the people, the source of political power.

And this brings us to consider the grounds on which it is contended that the Constitution establishes an indissoluble Union between the States.

1. It is said that the Constitution creates direct relations between the Government established by it and the individuals composing the United States – giving to the Government power to punish individuals for crimes committed against it; to impose taxes upon them and to collect the same; to require military service of them; and creating many other direct relations of duty and responsibility between the Government and the masses of the people, involving protection by the Government, and obedience and allegiance to its authority, on the part of individuals;

and that the Constitution was made and established, not as a compact between the States, but *by the people of the United States as one people.* It is hence contended that the Constitution created *a Government,* to which all the people composing the States are parties, as an aggregate mass, irrespective of the States; and that as to the authority and power of the Government, the people of all the States became one people, and the character of the States, as sovereign States, became extinguished or merged in the Union formed by the Constitution, which thereby became indissoluble by the acts of the several States.

Let us consider the arguments relied on to support these views.

In the first place, as to the parties which established the Constitution. Great reliance is placed upon the words of the preamble: *"We, the people of the United States,"* &c., as showing that it was the act of the people of the United States, as one people. But to this, there are several conclusive answers. 1st. The language is ambiguous, and, upon its face may as well mean the people of the United States *acting in their capacity as States,* as the people of the United States *as an aggregate mass;* for the language leaves it perfectly uncertain in what capacity "the people" were acting. It is evident that the words of themselves do not clearly sustain the argument founded on them; and at best they present a case of latent ambiguity. In such a case, we must resort to the history of the proceeding to ascertain the character in which "the people" acted, and the true import of the language used. And we learn from the entire history of the event – from the appointment of delegates to the General Convention – from the votes and proceedings of that Convention – from the proceedings of the several State Conventions of ratification – that every act in the formation and ratification of the Constitution, was done *by the States severally* and *in their political capacity.*

It is sufficient, on this point, to refer to the declarations of Mr. Madison, in the *Federalist*, No. 39. Speaking of the ratifications by the States, he says: "This assent and ratification is to be given by the people, *not as individuals composing an entire nation,* but as *composing the distinct and independent States to which they respectively belong.* * * * *Each State, in ratifying the Constitution, is considered as a sovereign body, independent of all others,* and only to be bound by its own voluntary act."

2d. The words of the preamble must be taken to refer to the condition of the States or people, *before,* and *at the time of, the ratification,* so far as they tend to designate the character of the parties to it; and it is admitted that the States were then sovereign States, *united by a compact,* and not one people called the United States. See Mr. Webster's speech on Mr. Calhoun's resolutions in February, 1833. So that there were then no *people of the United States,* in the sense of an aggregate mass or nation.

When the Constitution was submitted for ratification, there were no people of the United States, *under that Constitution.* The words under consideration cannot refer to the condition of the States or people, after the ratification; for upon no principle of construction, can general words – relating to the character in which parties to an instrument act – be referred to the *status* which they occupy under the operation of the instrument, but must be taken to designate the character in which they act at the time, and in the matter of the execution of the instrument. 3d. General words in a preamble cannot control an instrument so as to give it an operation contrary to its positive provisions, in opposition to the context and to all the facts attending its execution, showing the intention of the parties; and it is impossible to give to these words the effect contended for, without ignoring the plain intention of the framers of the Constitution and of the States in ratifying it, as shown by the entire history of these events.

We must, therefore resolve these doubtful words so as to make them consistent with truth, and expound them by the well known history of the events which gave rise to them; and so viewed, it appears to be impossible to escape the conclusion that they mean: *We, the people of the United States,* ACTING IN THE CAPACITY OF SOVEREIGN STATES, EACH FOR HERSELF.

The provisions of the Constitution are irreconcilable with the views insisted upon. They speak of "citizens of the different States" (Art. 3. Sec. 2), "the citizens of each State" (Art. 4. Sec 2); but nowhere of *citizens of the United States,* as would have been the case if the Constitution had been designed to establish a government of one entire people. No citizen of one State has the right to go into another State and there vote for any office, even for President of the United States, without becoming a citizen of that State, according to her constitution and laws.

In the next place, it is said that the Constitution establishes a *Government,* operating on all the individual citizens, and binding them to its authority, with ample powers to carry it into effect; and that this creates a *Government,* to which the people of the United States are parties, and a Union, which the States have no right to dissolve.

It is undoubtedly true that the Constitution empowers the Federal Government to exercise its legitimate jurisdiction directly over individuals; creating certain duties and obligations to be performed by them to the Government, and corresponding duties on the part of the Government to them. But it by no means follows that this power was derived from the act of the people of the United States, acting as independent individuals and irrespective of their condition as the people of the several States of which they were citizens. For it is above shown that all the acts in relation to the formation and ratification of the Constitution were done by the people of the States severally, in their sovereign capacity as political bodies. And the position here stated is but a repetition of that radical error which lies at the bottom of all the views in opposition to the true rights and powers of the States and the Federal Government, and in favor of the transcendent powers of the

Government of the United States.

    Nor does it follow from the fact that, in certain respects, the Federal Government has power to act upon individuals, that the States are thereby deprived of their sovereign powers. For, 1st, the great mass of their powers are expressly retained; and, as to all such, there could be no pretense that their powers of sovereignty were impaired by the delegation of the few powers in the Constitution. 2d, It is perfectly competent for a sovereign, by compact to grant to another, or to delegate to an agent, power to act directly upon his subject or citizen, in certain specified cases, without surrendering his sovereign rights and powers in other, and the most essential, attributes of sovereignty. And this may especially be done where there is a Confederate Union between two or more sovereigns, such as is referred to by Vattel in the citation above made; and of this character was the Federal Union under the Constitution of the United States. In such cases, the granted powers do not affect those not granted; the latter remaining as though the compact had never been made; and the determination of all questions in relation to the fact whether any particular power claimed, is granted or reserved, rests upon principles of public law applicable to the rights of sovereigns, where there is no common arbiter to judge between them; and each must judge for himself.

    2. It is said that the Constitution, and the laws and treaties, made in pursuance of it, are expressly ordained by the Constitution to be the *supreme law*

of the land; and that this deprives the States of all right and power to resume the powers of government delegated, under any circumstances, or to redress grievances under the action of the Government of the United States, except in the mode prescribed in the Constitution.

This position appears to be founded in a great misapprehension of the scope and purpose of the clause of the Constitution relied on to support it.

The Constitution and the laws and treaties made in pursuance of it, are, beyond doubt, the supreme law of the land; that is to say, they are paramount to the constitution and laws of the several States in all matters within the scope and limits of the powers delegated in the Constitution. But the object of the provision obviously was to prevent conflicts between the Constitution and laws of the Federal Government and those of the States, in *the ordinary administration of the delegated powers* of the Government. It established a rule of judicial and administrative action in such cases, without which the Government might have been powerless to execute its clearly delegated powers. But it has no reference whatever to questions of power between the States and Federal Government, arising by reason of the reserved rights of the States; and was never intended to have any application to those rights; for the manifest reason, that all such rights and powers were expressly retained, and were entirely beyond the sphere of action of the Federal Government as it was understood when the Constitution was adopted. Hence the provision can have no reference to the reserved rights and powers of the States.

That this is the true scope of this clause of the Constitution is plain from the observations of Mr. Madison, in relation to it in the 44th number of the *Federalist*. And Mr. Hamilton, says in No. 29, "that the laws of the Confederacy, *as to the enumerated and legitimate objects of its jurisdiction,* will become *the supreme law of the land.*"

But the construction attempted to be given to it would make the Constitution the supreme law in reference to matters not within its scope, and destroy rights and powers expressly reserved to the States by its provisions; or it begs the question, by assuming that the particular power in controversy is granted in the Constitution. It is, therefore, clear that it is not the supreme law in relation to the undelegated rights and powers of the States.

And here the important question arises – who is to determine controversies as to whether the acts of the Government are "in pursuance of" the Constitution – that is, whether they are in derogation of the reserved rights of the States?

It is insisted that the Supreme Court of the United States is the tribunal appointed by the Constitution to settle such questions; and to its decisions, that the States are bound to submit in all cases, since the Constitution confers upon that Court jurisdiction in *"all cases, in law and equity, arising under the Constitution, laws of the United States, and treaties made under the authority thereof."*

This, it is insisted, is the arbiter fixed for determining all questions of political power between the States and the Federal Government, except matters which cannot be resolved into the form of a suit; and in these, that the action of the Legislative department is conclusive as to its power to pass the acts.

If this view of the subject be well founded, it is clear that the Constitution makes a Government with very different powers from what was intended to be conferred. And does it not appear to be passing strange that the States should so positively reserve their rights and powers not delegated, and yet leave to the Federal Government the right of determining whether such and such rights were reserved or not – thereby making the Federal Government at once the judge, not only of its own powers, but of the rights and powers of the sovereign States composing the Union; in fact, placing all their rights and powers under the power and discretion of the Government, created for special and limited purposes? Jealous as were the States of their sovereign rights, and of the retention of them beyond the power of the Government formed by the Constitution – which is abundantly shown, both in the history of the proceedings of the Convention which formed it, and of the State Conventions in ratifying it – it is impossible to believe that they could have intended to confer on the Government, through one of its departments, a power which would enable it to enlarge its powers at discretion, to the virtual destruction of their essential rights and powers as sovereign States. And it may be safely asserted, upon the history referred to, that if any such power had been claimed for Congress, or if any such construction had been put upon the clause in relation to the Judicial Department, as is contended for, the Constitution would have been prompt-ly rejected or the misconception prevented by amendment. The statesmen of that day knew too well the history of judicial usurpations in England, and everywhere else, to entrust the cherished rights of the States to a tribunal so prone to enlarge the just sphere of governmental powers.

It may be remarked, with reference to the position that Congress is the judge of its own powers, that it would have been useless to give to the judiciary the power to determine such questions, if that position be sound. And if the power be given to the judiciary, that is sufficient to show that it was not intended to be given to Congress. The argument in favor of the former refutes that in favor of the latter. It is also clear, that this doctrine would make the discretion of Congress, and not the limitations of the Constitution, the boundary of its power, and would virtually transform the Government into one of unlimited powers.

But the authority claimed for the Supreme Court is more relied on, and is entitled to more consideration.

The reasons for the jurisdiction given to the judiciary by this provision are stated to be:

1st. To supply the defect in the Articles of Confederation, and provide a tribunal to give uniformity of construction to the laws passed by Congress and treaties made in relation to matters clearly within the jurisdiction of the Government; and to prevent the confusion that would arise from divers constructions, in such cases, by the several State Courts (see *Federalist*, No. 22, page 102 and No. 80, page 365). 2d. To restrain the States from the exercise of powers prohibited to them by the Constitution (*ibid.*, No. 80, page 365-367.

    These are stated by the advocates of the Constitution – who were participants in its formation and intimately acquainted with the intention with which its provisions were framed – to be the scope and object of the clause. Mr. Hamilton said, "It seems scarcely to admit of controversy, that the judiciary authority of the Union ought to extend to these several descriptions of cases: 1st, To all those which arise out of the laws of the United States, *passed in pursuance of their just and Constitutional powers of legislation.* 2d. To all those which concern the extension of the provisions expressly contained in the Articles of Union. 3d. To all those in which the United States are a party. 4th. To all those which involve the power of the Confederacy, whether they relate to the intercourse between the United States and foreign nations, or to that between the States themselves. 5th. To all those which originate on the high seas and are of admiralty, or maritime jurisdiction; and, lastly, to all those in which the State tribunals cannot be supposed to be impartial and unbiased" (*ibid.*, No. 80).

The first class, he says, has reference to restrictions placed by the Constitution on the powers of the States, in matters prohibited to them, and is justified on the ground of providing "a Constitutional method of giving efficiency to Constitutional provisions," and of exercising powers clearly granted to the Government. The second class is justified on the ground of necessity in giving uniformity to the laws of the Government passed in pursuance of their legitimate powers. The third has reference to controversies between the nation and its members or citizens; the fourth, to the determination of *causes* between two States, between one State and the citizens of another, and between the citizens of different States; the fifth, to the special cases mentioned; and the sixth, to causes of a civil nature between different States and their citizens in which the State courts may be supposed to be biased.

It is to the first two classes above enumerated, that the clauses of the Constitution, in relation to *cases in law and equity arising under the Constitution and the laws of the United States,* is applicable, as Mr. Hamilton distinctly states. He asks what is meant by *"cases arising under the Constitution;"* and answers, that it *refers to restrictions upon the authority of the State Legislatures, and to their exercise of powers prohibited to them by the Constitution.* Strong advocate as he was, in his individual opinions, of a Government of large powers, he gives no countenance to the idea – in stating the principles and objects of the Constitution – that the clause under consideration had any reference to questions *of political power* arising between the States and the Federal Government. Neither the words of the clause – "*cases* in law or equity arising *under* the Constitution" – nor the contemporaneous exposition given to it by its advocates, justify the construction attempted to be given to them. And it is perfectly clear from the history of the Constitution, and from the well known jealousy of the States in regard to the danger of an undue extension of the powers of the Government in its course and progress, that it was never contemplated to confer upon the Government created by them, the power to determine and circumscribe their reserved rights and powers, and through one of its departments to enlarge its own powers according to judicial discretion. That history affords the most ample evidence that the States could never have intended to make the Federal Government the judge of their reserved rights and powers; and that the Constitution would never have been ratified if it had contained any such doctrine, in regard to the powers of the Government and the jurisdiction of the Supreme Court, as that sanctioned by that Court in the case of *McCulloch vs. the State of Maryland*. No such power was claimed for it until long after it had been in operation, nor until its genius and spirit had been seriously perverted by ingenious constructions and false theories which have finally ended in its subversion.

It is, therefore, evident that the power is not granted to the Federal Government to determine questions of this nature, and thereby to preclude the rights of the States.

But suppose the Federal Government usurps powers in a form which cannot be brought before the judiciary; or suppose the judgment of the Supreme Court, in favor of the rights of a State. be disregarded by the Executive and Legislative departments of the Government, which persist in the unconstitutional acts to the oppression of the people of the States. Is there no remedy? Every man must answer that there is; or the sacred rights of self-protection and of self-government are vain and illusory, and the Constitution of the United States erects a despotism under the guise of a Federal Republic. What, then, is the nature of the remedy? *Is it a matter of right,* or does it depend upon the mere ability of the State to maintain it to a successful issue if resisted by force?

It must be matter of right; because, by the violation of the compact of Union to her oppression, she had the right to consider the compact as at an end, and was remitted to her original sovereign rights, if she thought fit to resume them; and this right necessarily arose from the nature of the compact, which was a *Federal Union* for specific purposes to a limited extent between *the States as sovereign parties to it.* And this is *the right of secession – a right;* and therefore beyond the rightful molestation or interference of any earthly power.

If this be not true, her rights are violated and the compact of Union subverted to her oppression, and yet she has no other remedy than to resist the usurpation by force – the remedy of revolution, which is only rightful, in the estimation of the world, when it becomes successful; and, if unsuccessful, is rebellion and treason. Under this view, she has no *right* to avoid or resist the usurpation and oppression; but her right depends upon whether she can successfully maintain herself against the oppressor – and that is no right at all – so that the strange case is presented of a clear wrong and usurpation, by one party, to the oppression of the other, without any absolute and adequate right of redress to the latter, except that of brute force. Then she either has no right at all in such a case, or she has the right to treat the compact as ended by the violation of its provisions, and to be restored to her position of an absolutely sovereign State, which she enjoyed before the Union was formed – which is the right of secession.

To illustrate further – suppose an act of the Federal Government, in gross and palpable violation of the positive guaranties, or powers prohibited to the Government in the Constitution, operating to the oppression of a single State; and suppose none of the other States would co-operate with her in resisting it – it is plain that if the Federal Government thought fit to persist in enforcing it, the State would be without remedy, unless she had the right to absolve herself from the Union. The remedy of revolution would only lead to her destruction by overwhelming forces. Has she then no higher right than that of mere force to resist the oppression? Unquestionably, from the nature of the compact between her and her associate States in the Union, she has the right to withdraw from the confederacy, and peaceably to resume her position as a sovereign and independent State, because this was a right appertaining to her as a sovereign State, and which she had never surrendered in the Constitution.

The distinction between *secession* and *revolution* is not merely in terms. It is wide and essential. The former is founded in right, and does not depend on force for its complete enjoyment. Being rightful, no power on earth has a right to gainsay it, or to interfere with its exercise; for there cannot be conflicting rights upon one and the same subject. Because the State entered into the Union as a sovereignty, and retained all her sovereign powers which she did not delegate to the Government, upon the violation of the fundamental conditions of the compact, she was absolved from its obligations, and restored to all her sovereign powers.

But *revolution,* as a means of redress, is a mere forcible resistance to wrong and oppression under a constituted government, from which it assumes there is no legal right to be absolved – to be met by opposing force. *It is not predicable of the right to resume the former position of a sovereign State.* If successful, the State is delivered from the oppression, *but does not thereby necessarily become restored to her status as a sovereign State.* If her resistance is unsuccessful, it is treason and rebellion. But secession, being the act of the State in her sovereign capacity as a party to the compact, is founded on her reserved right of sovereignty, and results from the dissolution of the compact; and whether successful or not, it is, in law but the exercise of *a political right.* Her people, in defending her position, are guilty of no offence, but are in the performance of the highest duty of patriotism; and those who assail her by violence, in the exercise of her right, are guilty of wrong before the nations of the earth, unless her legal right be exercised in bad faith and unjustifiably, to the injury of her associates in the Union.

Another objection to the right of secession is, that the remedy for abuses and violations of the Constitution is prescribed in the provision for amendments.

But that does not impair the right to "alter or abolish" a Government, and "to institute a new Government," set forth in the Declaration of Independence. It has reference to such amendments as might be found necessary by time and experience, and which might be agreed on, in the regular action of the Government. But it imports no obligation never to abolish or abandon it, and never to form a new Government. The 13th Article of Confederation, expressly declared that the Union thereby created should be perpetual, and prohibited any alteration of the Articles except in a prescribed mode. That is stronger in its terms than the Article relative to Amendments in the Constitution of the United States, which simply provides a mode of making Amendments; whereas the former emphatically *prohibited* any alteration except in the mode prescribed.

Yet this was disregarded and the Constitution of the United States formed, establishing a totally different Government, abolishing the old one; and all this, in a mode entirely different from that required in the Articles of Confederation, against the consent of several of the States. This was justified at the time, on the ground of the high and sacred right of the States to alter or abolish their Government, as we have above shown.

So the State constitutions contain provisions prescribing the mode of amending them; but this has never been held to debar the exercise of the sovereign right of the people of the State to form a new constitution in a different mode from that prescribed; and many of the State constitutions now existing, were formed in that manner.

But it may be impracticable to amend the Constitution in the mode prescribed, by reason of the circumstances, and the growth of usurpations; or it may have become perverted to the destruction of the rights intended to be secured when it was made, beyond remedy by amendment in the mode prescribed – so that the remedy by amendment would be impracticable or inadequate in such cases. And that is the condition in which the Southern States were placed, when they were compelled to secede.

It is a matter of history, that all efforts to obtain protection for their clear Constitutional rights were spurned and rejected by an unscrupulous majority of Congress, with insult and menaces that they would consummate the outrages which were sought to be prevented by proposed amendments.

There was, therefore, no alternative left them, but to give up their most sacred rights, or take their protection into their own hands by withdrawing from a Union which was to be made the instrument of their oppression and ruin.

Having thus considered the arguments mainly relied on in opposition to the right of secession, let us bring the theory which denies the right to a practical test by the cardinal principles of the Constitution. If a State have not the right to withdraw from the Union under any circumstances, she must be bound to submit to its power and the United States must have the right to coerce her to submission; and if the United States have not that right, it must be because the State has the right to withdraw; for wherever there is a right there is a remedy. If the withdrawal be without right, the remedy would be to reduce her to submission by force. If she persisted, it would produce war, and she could only be kept in the Union by conquest, and only held in submission to the authority of the United States by military force. She is then reduced to the condition of a subjugated State, and ceases to be a member of the Union composed of equal States.

Now the Union formed by the Constitution – and the only Union that can subsist under it – was one of equal sovereign States. It was established "in order to form a more perfect Union, establish justice and ensure domestic tranquility," between its members. All the provisions of the Constitution show that equality of rights and of political condition is indispensable to its existence. But this fundamental condition is utterly subverted by the necessary effect of military coercion; for instead of a co-equal member of the Union, the State becomes a subjugated and degraded province; and, instead of her people having a government of their own choice and resting upon their own consent, they are held under the forcible dominion of the Government of the United States.

This is the plain result of the denial of the right of secession, and of the assertion of the right to hold a State in the Union against her will. It dissolves the Union so far as the subjugated State is concerned as effectually as secession, and in a manner that would utterly prostrate every principle of American liberty, and with consequences shocking to every feeling of patriotism and even of humanity. It deposes the legitimate governmental authorities of the State, and erects, in their place, a Government of force, deriving its authority not from the people of the State, the only proper source of political power, but from the arms of the conqueror. The State Government is subverted, and the people are held in subjection to a military despotism, as Mr. Hamilton said would be the result of such a policy. The State ceases to be one of the free and sovereign States, and as such to form a constituent part of the American Union; and the Union is dissolved by the destruction of her proper political condition as perfectly as it could have been by secession, and in a mode and by means as much more abhorrent to justice and to American principles, as a Government established and sustained by force is worse than one established by the people themselves; which – though unwise, it may be, in its organization – yet rests on the solid foundation of the consent of those for whose happiness it is instituted and by whose consent alone it can subsist.

But if there could be a reasonable doubt on this point, it is removed by the history of the Constitution, and the declarations of its advocates when it was submitted for ratification.

It was a material defect in the Articles of Confederation that there was no authority to enforce the acts of Congress against the States. It was fully admitted, by the fathers of the Constitution, that it would be an anomaly, in a Government composed of sovereign States, to attempt to compel obedience to the laws by force employed against the States in their political capacity; because it would necessarily result in war against the power of the State, which would dissolve the Union. Mr. Hamilton said, "the first war of this kind would probably terminate in the dissolution of the Union;" and further, "*such a scheme,* if practicable at all, *would instantly degenerate into a military despotism;* but it will be found in every light impracticable" (*Federalist*, No. 16, pages 72, 73).

Mr. Madison says, "As it is a solecism in theory, so in practice, it is subversion of the order and end of civil polity, by substituting violence in the place of law, or the destructive *coercion of the sword* in place of the mild and salutary *coercion of the magistracy*" (*ibid.*, No. 20, page 92).

It being wholly inadmissible to coerce *the States* by force of arms, the plan proposed by the Constitution was to operate upon *the individual citizens* of the State "*through the medium of the courts, by giving the Federal Government the same advantage for securing obedience to its authority, which is enjoyed by the government of each State*" (*ibid.*, Nos. 15 and 27. And this in the whole extent of the power of coercion proposed to be given to the Government – *the power to compel obedience from individuals by process of law.*

So long as the resistance to the acts of the Federal Government was confined to mere individuals, the authority of the United States might extend to them, to compel them to obedience in the modes recognized by law. But when a State withdraws from the Union and resumes her position as an independent sovereign State, she is in the same condition, at least, as that she occupied before the Constitution was ratified. Her citizens are bound to support her government, under penalties for disloyalty to be enforced by the authority of the State; which places them in the position of refusing obedience to the authority of the United States, not as individuals, but under the command and sanction of the State, in whom the original and inherent sovereignty resides; the State in her sovereign character, in virtue of her reserved right, has asserted her paramount authority over them, and their action is in obedience to that authority. There arises then, a conflict between the State in her sovereign capacity, and the United States; and to proceed against an individual acting under such sanctions, would be a manifest violation of the spirit of the Constitution. But the controversy is between the State in her political capacity and the Government of the United States. This is clear; because if the United States attempt to enforce their authority over the individual, it is met by the protection of the State, and a conflict of forces must be the result. It is not, therefore, within the reason which conferred the power upon the United States.

Mr. Hamilton pointedly refers to this contingency in No. 16, *Federalist*, as follows:

"If opposition to the national government should arise from the disorderly conduct of refractory or seditious individuals, it could be overcome by the same means which are employed against the same evil under the State government. * * * As to those partial commotions and insurrections, which sometimes disquiet society, from the intrigues of an inconsiderable faction, or from sudden or occasional ill-humors, that do not infect the great body of the community, the General Government could command more extensive resources, for the suppression of disturbances of that kind, than would be in the power of a single member. And as to these mortal feuds which, in certain conjunctures, spread a conflagration through the whole nation, or through a very large proportion of it, proceeding either from weighty causes of discontent, given by the Government, or from the contagion of some violent popular paroxysm, they do not fall within any ordinary rules of calculation. When they happen, they commonly amount to revolutions and dismemberments of empire."

It is abundantly clear that the right of coercion against one of the States was never asserted by the framers of the Constitution, nor contemplated in its ratification by the States; but was expressly disavowed by both. It is utterly repugnant to the genius and spirit of the Constitution. Indeed the total inadmissibility of employing force against States – the very essence of whose Union was peace and concord, unity of feeling and of interest – was one of the reasons most strongly urged for the adoption of a system to act upon individuals, as we have above seen; and the same reason applies, in all its force, to the Union under the Constitution.

Mr. Hamilton, in the Convention of ratification of New York – speaking of the proposition to coerce the States to comply with the requisitions for revenue, under the Articles of Confederation – expressed his objections to it in the following language, which is applicable, with equal force, to the coercion of States under the present Constitution:

"It has been observed, *to coerce the States is one of the maddest projects that was ever devised.* A failure of compliance will never be confined to a single State. This being the case, can we suppose it wise to hazard a civil war? Suppose Massachusetts or any large State should refuse, and Congress should attempt to compel them; would they not have influence to procure assistance, especially from those States who are in the same situation as themselves? What picture does this idea present to our view? A complying State at war with a non-complying State: Congress marching the troops of one State into the bosom of another: this State collecting auxiliaries and forming perhaps a majority against its federal head. *Here is a nation at war with itself. Can any reasonable man be well disposed toward a government which makes war and carnage the only means of supporting itself?* Every such war must involve the innocent with the guilty. This single consideration should be sufficient to dispose every peaceable citizen against such a government" (2 Elliott's *Debates*, 232).

In the Convention which formed the Constitution, he said – upon the proposition of Mr. Randolph to give the power to the Federal Government to use force against a State – that *"it would produce a dissolution of the Union"* (2 *Madison Papers*, 881).

And these are the declarations of the great master spirt of the advocates of latitudinous powers in the Federal Government.

Mr. Madison said upon the same proposition, "that the more he reflected on the use of force, the more he doubted the practicability, the justice and the efficiency of it, when applied to the people collectively, and not individually. *A Union of the States, containing such an ingredient, seemed to pro-*

SECESSION 47

vide for its own destruction. The use of force against a State would look more like a declaration of war, than an infliction of punishment, and would probably be considered by THE PARTY ATTACKED *as a dissolution of all previous compacts by which it might be bound.*" And, on his motion, the proposition was *unanimously* postponed (2 *Madison Papers*, 761). And it was not afterwards revived.

It is, therefore, impossible to maintain the right of coercion against a State without turning a deaf ear to the history of the Constitution, and destroying the very foundation on which the Union rests. And it must follow, that if there is no right to compel a State to remain in the Union, there can be no right to demand her continuance in it against her will; and, hence, that in point of political power, she has the right to secede from it.

Upon these considerations, it is confidently submitted to the dispassionate judgment of mankind, that the right of secession, as exercised by the several Southern States of the late American Union, was a clear and unquestionable sovereign right appertaining to those States.

TWO
☆ ☆ ☆ ☆

We come now to examine the *grounds of justification* for the secession of the Southern States.

In order to a just understanding of this question it is necessary to take a cursory view of the state of political parties, as they affected the condition of this country at the time of the dissolution of the Union.

It was not long after the Government of the United States went into operation under the Constitution before a strong party sprang up, claiming for it powers wholly inconsistent with its true spirit and intent, and especially with the reserved rights of the States. This party numbered many men of eminent talents, who had borne a prominent part in the war of the Revolution, whose influence gave to their doctrines great force among the people, and enabled them to impress their views upon the character of the Government by various legislative acts of doubtful constitutionality.

From natural causes, and under the operation

of these measures from time to time enacted, it became apparent that the chief interests and pursuits of the States were different, and, for the most part, sectional; the one section being commercial and manufacturing, and the other agricultural; the former being composed of the Eastern and Northern States, and latter of the Southern and Western States.

These measures and the doctrines on which some of them were founded, gave rise to the party above referred to, known as the Federal party, which had its opponent in what was called the Democratic or Republican party; the former claiming large and extensive powers for the Federal Government, and the latter seeking to confine it within the strict limits of the terms of the Constitution. The strength of the Federal party lay mainly in the Eastern and Northern section, while that of the other lay mostly in the Southern and Western section.

In the progress of the Government, the latter became the dominant party; and finally, and especially after the war of 1812 with Great Britain, the Federal party became so unpopular, that its prospects of attaining the ascendant again were almost hopeless. But the debt of that war gave rise to measures of finance and revenue which, in a manner, gave countenance to their political doctrines, while they contributed greatly to their pecuniary benefit in promoting their commerce and manufactures, to the detriment of the other section. This revived the hopes of the Federal party. Their politicians were encouraged in their hopes to attain to the honors and power of the Government, and their people rejoiced in the prospect of profit and emolument by the action of the Government giving advantages to their interests and pursuits which could not be enjoyed by the other section, by reason of the nature of their pursuits. Having the strong motives of the *lust of power,* and the *lust of gain* to stimulate them, they entered upon deep-laid schemes to recover from their fall, and to secure both these ends.

But the advantage which they derived from the unequal action of these measures in their favor was not sufficient to assure the success of their purposes. The South and the West were strongly opposed to their political principles, and to the policy of the measures which operated so unjustly to their own pecuniary advantage. It would be with difficulty that they could obtain success for their party, even in the States then composing the Union; but this success was utterly hopeless if new States were added to the Union composed of the territories and public domain then belonging to the United States. It was from that quarter alone, with the exception of Maine, that new States could be added to the Union; and it was perfectly evident that such States – having the same interests and entertaining the same political principles as their neighboring States, and all being agricultural and injuriously affected by the policy which operated to the benefit of the Eastern and Northern section – would, in all human probability, be opposed to the politicians and policy of the Federal party.

They, therefore, conceived the design to prevent the admission of any new States into the Union from that quarter. The same motive had caused their opposition to the purchase of Louisiana, and subsequently caused the fierce war which they waged against the annexation of Texas. But it would never do to avow such a purpose openly, since the admission of new States was expressly contemplated in the Constitution; and this Western and Southern territory was the section from which they were to come. It was, therefore, necessary to disguise their design under some plausible pretext; and, with characteristic Jesuitism, they seized upon philanthropy for the purpose.

African slavery was then a part of the domestic policy of the these South-Western and Southern States; and it would, at that time, have been absolutely ruinous to new States to be made of the territory adjacent to them to be deprived of slave labor in their agricultural pursuits, and to be admitted only on condition that it was excluded within their limits. Hence to require such a condition was in fact to exclude the State from the Union; and that was the real design. It was believed, by the contrivers of this plot, that such was the prejudice then existing in the sentiment of most of the civilized nations of the earth, and even in this country, against Negro slavery, that their odious motive would be concealed under the cloak of benevolence and philanthropy, whilst they secured the power and honors of the Government, and employed them for their emolument.

SECESSION

The first State which applied for admission after these purposes were conceived was the State of Missouri; and this furnished the first opportunity to the party to put into practice the scheme which they had planned. All their strength was accordingly put forth to prevent the admission of the State, except upon the condition of exclusion of slavery within her limits – a condition destructive to the rights of a large number of her people, ruinous to her settled policy and interests, and of course wholly impracticable to be accepted; and a flagrant violation of the Constitution, as has since been adjudged by the Supreme Court of the United States. Yet they urged it with all their power and with unyielding obstinacy; and the memorable struggle ensued which brought the Union to the verge of destruction. They persisted in their demand until the destruction of the Union or the rejection of the condition was the inevitable alternative; and, even under these awful circumstances, they only agreed to recede from their position in the particular case, by obtaining another condition, declaring as the settled policy of the Government, in effect, that slavery should never exist in any of the Western States to be created out of the territory in that section – a principle which they believed would exclude from the Union a large number of agricultural States to be made out of the Western territory, whose interests and political principles would be opposed to their own. But for this unconscientious advantage, it is plain that these wicked men would then have dissolved the Union.

They, therefore, agreed to admit Missouri, under the belief, that the condition, which they had succeeded in obtaining, would accomplish their object of excluding all other Western agricultural territories, which, in the course of a few years, would apply for admission as States, and which would be, for the most part, in the situation of Missouri in regard to slavery, and so deeply interested in slave labor that they would not accept admission with its exclusion; and hence that they would not be admitted.

This was the effect which they thought would most probably be produced by the arrangement. But if this failed, they expected to obtain the end desired by them by indirection and by the operation of this policy; which was, that the Legislative declaration excluding slavery, under the so called Missouri Compromise, from these Western territories would prevent the immigration there of people of the slave-holding States, with their slaves, and that the public domain would be open to the people of the Eastern and Northern States for settlement – thereby enabling them to monopolise the rich lands of that region to their pecuniary emolument, and to people them with a population of their own political opinions, who would coalesce with them and enable them to hold the political power, and to control the policy of the country in favor of their own doctrines and schemes.

Having gained these important advantages over the constitutional rights of the South, they were willing to await their development, confident of ultimately reaping the fruits of such well laid plans.

John Q. Adams, a leading man of their section, was then Secretary of State; and, being thus "in the line of safe precedents," was expected to become President of the United States in a few years; by which time all their schemes of power and emolument would be ripe, and under whose administration they would receive their full fruition. Meanwhile a political calm pervaded the country, which terminated in the election of Mr. Adams in 1825. True to his section and to his party instincts, he did not disappoint their expectation; and during his administration, measures were passed giving benefits and advantages to the interests and pursuits of that section, to the utmost of their demands, and operating most unjustly and oppressively to the interests and pursuits of the South and West. These measures aroused a deep feeling of opposition in the latter section; and this, in connection with the fraudulent combination by which it was believed Mr. Adams was chosen President, by the House of Representatives, and the strong-government doctrines which characterized his administration, rendered him so odious, that he was overwhelmingly defeated in 1828. He and his party were driven from power, and appeared to be prostrated to rise no more.

During this period of their realization of the power and emoluments of the Government, there was no necessity to agitate questions to produce discord and confusion. But this was quickly changed when they were expelled from the power and patronage of the Government. With a perseverance known only to a thirst for political power, stimulated by the lust of gain, this party aroused itself from its prostration, and armed itself for a new and terrific conflict, a death struggle, to rule or ruin the country; and the weapon chosen for this warfare was the same slavery question which had been so valuable to them in their previous efforts. It had lain dormant while they were in power reaping the emoluments of a Government perverted to their profit; but now in their fallen and degraded state – employing it always *as a means* to power and gain, and never *as an end* – it became necessary to brandish it again in all its horrors in order to rise again. Mr. Adams was sent to Congress, the chosen man of the party; and, reckless of decency and of the dignity which his recent position would have suggested to a man of juster sensibilities, he quickly began the agitation of the slavery question, with all the violence which disappointed personal ambition and thirst for power, the prostration of his sectional party and the defeat of their schemes for ill gotten gain, could give to a man of untiring energy, of great abilities and of the deepest malignity. His effort was to stab, in its vitals, that section which had directed against him the blow that had felled and degraded him, and was about to deprive his section of its unconscientious gains; and he scrupled at nothing which he could use as a means of wreaking his revenge. Incessantly did he exert himself, by appeals to false sympathy and to hypocritical philanthropy, and by ingenious sophistries, to arouse the spirit of fanaticism in behalf of the happy and contented slaves of the South. At first his efforts met with no favor. This but incited him to greater exertions. He found coadjutors in Congress. His spirit was communicated to leading men throughout his section, and to many in the West who had emigrated from that section or who had been corrupted by his Jesuitism. It was then found that the Missouri Compromise had worked its office, and would add to the Northern and Eastern faction the new States to be made of Western territory, by preventing the immigration of Southern men with their slaves there, and that those States would ultimately be added to their party; and hence it was no longer necessary to oppose the admission of new States from that region. The party increased in numbers from year to year, until all the Eastern and North-Eastern States, and a large majority of the Western States – which were peopled for the most part by men of Eastern and Northern birth and by foreigners – were enlisted under its banner. They avowed themselves prepared to trample under foot the principles of the Constitution; their Legislatures passed acts deliberately annulling a positive provision of the Constitution for the rendition of fugitive slaves, and setting at nought the act of Congress passed in furtherance of that provision; and these outrageous acts they persisted in carrying out even by force; and in the Presidential election of 1860, the votes of those States, constituting a large majority of the States of the Union, were cast for Abraham Lincoln, who was openly pledged to use all the powers of the Government to put an end to slave property in the States, and to prevent its existence in the Territories – *rights clearly recognised in the Constitution; adjudged by the Supreme Court to be guarantied by the Constitution; considered vital to the welfare and happiness of fifteen States of the Union – rights, without the recognition of which in the Constitution, the Union could never have been formed.*

    Throughout all the stages of these efforts, the Southern States solemnly warned their authors of their inevitable result, if pressed by them; and by all that was dear in private right, all that was sacred under the solemn sanctions of the Constitution – by all that was beloved and venerated in the glorious institutions which were established by our ancestors and committed to us as a precious boon to be kept in its virtue and purity, and transmitted to posterity – in all the forms of reasoning, of entreaty and of expostulation, these men were implored to desist from their efforts, and not to force the South to the dread necessity of dissolving that Union which was their pride and their glory. These solemn warnings were only met by insult and defiance; and steadily the enemies of the Constitution and of the liberties of the South advanced to the consummation of their purposes, until in the language of Mr. Seward, their chief leader, on the eve of Mr. Lincoln's election, they were *"in the last stage of the conflict, before the* GREAT TRIUMPHAL INAUGURATION *of this policy into the Government of the United States."*

In order to estimate the danger threatened to these States by the accession of Abraham Lincoln to the power of the Federal Government, and by their remaining under his dominion, it is proper to set forth the principles and designs upon which he and his party were to come into power, and the especial object of their elevation. This is written in characters that it would have been madness to disregard.

In the authorized publication of Mr. Lincoln's speeches, circulated during his presidential canvass, the speeches from which the following extracts are made, will be found.

"*I believe this Government cannot endure permanently half slave and half free.* I do not expect the Union to be dissolved. I do not expect the house to fall. I do expect it will cease to be divided. *It will become all one thing or all the other.* Either the opponents of slavery will arrest the further spread of it, and place it where the public mind shall rest in the belief that it is *in the course of ultimate extinction,* or its advocates will push it forward till it shall become alike lawful in all the States."

Commenting on this, he afterwards said, "I only said what *I expected* would take place. I did not even say that I desired that slavery shall be put in the course of ultimate extinction. I DO NOW, HOWEVER; so there need be no longer any difficulty about that."

"If I were in Congress and a vote should come up on a question whether slavery should be prohibited in a new Territory, *in spite of the Dred Scott de-*

cision, I would vote that it should."

"What I do say is, that no man is good enough to govern another man without the other man's consent. *I say this is the leading principle, the sheet anchor of American Republicanism.*"

After quoting a passage from the Declaration of Independence, he says, "I have quoted so much at this time merely to show, that according to our ancient faith, the powers of government are derived from the consent of the governed. Now, the relation of master and slave is, *pro tanto*, a violation of this principle. The master not only governs the slave, without his consent, but he governs him by a set of rules altogether different from those which he prescribes himself. *Allow all the governed an equal voice in the government; and that, and that only, is self-government.*"

Mr. Seward declared the principles and purposes of the party, as follows – speaking of the antagonism between free labor and slave labor, he said:

"IT IS AN IRREPRESSIBLE CONFLICT between the opposing and enduring forces, and it means that the United States must and will, sooner or later, become entirely a slave-holding nation, or entirely a free-labor nation. Either the cotton and rice fields of South Carolina and the sugar plantations of Louisiana will ultimately be tilled by free labor, and Charleston and New Orleans become marts for legitimate merchandise alone, or else the rye-fields and wheat fields of Massachusetts and New York must again be surrendered by their farmers to slave culture, and to the production of slaves, and Boston and New York become once more a market for trade in the bodies and souls of men."

Again, he says: "What a commentary upon the history of man is the fact, that eighteen years after the death of John Quincy Adams, the *people have for their standard-bearer, Abraham Lincoln, confessing the obligations of* THE HIGHER LAW, which the sage of Quincy proclaimed, and *contending for weal or woe, for life or death, in the irrepressible conflict between freedom and slavery.* I desire only to say that WE ARE IN THE LAST STAGE OF THE CONFLICT, BEFORE THE GREAT TRIUMPHAL INAUGURATION OF THIS POLICY INTO THE GOVERNMENT OF THE UNITED STATES."

Speaking of the decision of the Supreme Court in the case of Dred Scott, he says:

"The people of the United States never can, and they never will, accept principles so unconstitutional and so abhorrent. Never – never. *Let the Court recede.* Whether it recedes or not, we shall reorganize the Court, and thus reform its political sentiments and practices."

"It is written *in the Constitution of the United States, in violation of the divine law,* that we shall surrender the fugitive slave. You blush not at these things because they are familiar as household words."

Mr. Chase, a leading man of the party, and now Secretary of the Treasury, proclaimed the same views. He said:

"We feel, therefore, that *all legal distinction between individuals of the same community, founded on any such circumstances as color, origin and the like, are hostile to the genius of our institutions, and incompatible with the true theory of American liberty. Slavery and oppression must cease or American liberty must perish.*"

"I embrace, with pleasure, this opportunity of declaring my disapprobation of that clause of the Constitution which denies to a portion of the colored people the right of suffrage."

"For myself, I am ready to renew my pledge, and I will venture to *speak in behalf of my co-workers,* that *we will go straight on, without faltering or wavering, until every vestige of oppression shall be erased from the statute-books – until the sun, in all its journey from the utmost Eastern horizon though the mid-heaven, till he sinks behind the Western bed,* SHALL NOT BEHOLD THE FOOT PRINT OF A SINGLE SLAVE IN ALL OUR BROAD AND GLORIOUS LAND."

The seventh resolution of the Chicago Convention, which nominated Mr. Lincoln, sets forth the doctrines of the party in these words:

"7. That the *new dogma,* that the Constitution of its own force, carries slavery into the territories of the United States, is *a dangerous political heresy*, at variance with the explicit provisions of that instrument itself, with contemporaneous exposition, and with legislative and judicial precedent; is revolutionary in its tendency, and subversive of the peace and harmony of the country."

And this is said with reference to a solemn decision of the Supreme Court of the United States, which is treated as a mere dogma, and *denounced as a political heresy* entitled to no force with the authorities about to take upon themselves the administration of the Government of the United States! And what makes it still more flagrant is, that it comes from the leaders of a party which had always so strenuously asserted the binding force of the decisions of the Supreme Court upon questions relating to the powers of the Government!

The advocates and party press throughout the country, which supported Mr. Lincoln, proclaimed the same principles and purposes as the ground on which he was supported; and after his election, they, with one accord, rejoiced that the voice of the people had crowned their efforts with success, and invested them with the high duty of prostrating the guaranties of the Constitution.

While these principles and designs were proclaimed in the presidential contest, the Southern States again solemnly warned the advocates of them that they could never submit to a Government administered with such purposes, and that a dissolution of the Union would be the necessary result of the accession of Mr. Lincoln unless adequate guaranties were given for the protection of their rights. Many of them thought the prospect of obtaining such guaranties hopeless; and that the election of Mr. Lincoln, upon the declaration of principles and purposes on which he was elected, was the *proclamation of a revolution* in the Government; and that it was their duty to act promptly for their own protection, and withdraw in their sovereign capacities from the Union. Others were reluctant to take that step until every effort to obtain security had been exhausted, or until the administration of Mr. Lincoln should show, by some overt act, that the avowed designs of his party were to be carried into execution.

Acting on the latter view, the resolutions of Mr. Crittenden were introduced into the Senate in December, 1860. These resolutions demanded nothing but the clear and unquestionable rights of the Southern States under the Constitution, and conceded much of principle and settled right on their part, which nothing but a deep reverence for the Union and a fervent desire to prevent its dissolution – if that could be done consistently with their indispensable rights – could have reconciled them to yield. Among these concessions was the constitutional right – which had been adjudged by the Supreme Court and was therefore settled – of taking their slaves to the Territories of the United States, north of 36 deg. 30 min.; which was proposed to be surrendered without the surrender of any settled right or constitutional privilege on the part of the Northern States, and without any equivalent to the South. These resolutions – which, all just minds must admit, evince, in a high degree, the spirit of concession and self-sacrifice which animated the Southern States in order to save the Union, were referred to a committee of thirteen, composed of members representing the three parties in the country: Republicans, Conservatives and Secessionists. The two last – among whom was the President of the Confederate States – expressed their willingness to accept the settlement proposed, if the first would accede to it; for without the support of them and of their party, it would be useless, since it was obvious that the adjustment would be nugatory without the sanction of the party which they represented. But on the 22d December, 1860, they declared that *"these questions had been settled by the people at the late Presidential election, and that they had no concessions to make or offer."*

    This declaration, made under the most solemn circumstances, showed conclusively that the designs of the party of Mr. Lincoln, as declared in the Presidential canvass, were to be carried out, and that the rights of the Southern States, under the positive provisions of the Constitution, were to be trampled under foot, and that that was considered as settled at the ballot box.

    This was soon followed by the vote on the resolutions in the Senate – when every Senator of Mr. Lincoln's party voted against them – and by the action of the Peace Conference, assembled at the instance of the State of Virginia, with a view, if possible, to render the constitutional rights of the South safe, and to restore harmony to the country.

    All these efforts on the part of the Southern States signally failed to obtain from the party of Mr.

Lincoln any assurances or guaranties whatever that the power of the Government would not be employed to consummate the schemes of violation of the rights of the Southern States, proclaimed by his party during the Presidential canvass.

Indeed, the tone and conduct of the entire party clearly manifested that they considered that the *fiat* had gone forth from the ballot box at the recent election, and that the edict only remained to be executed. They announced throughout the land *"the great triumphal inauguration of this policy"* of trampling under foot the clear and unquestioned rights of the people of the slaveholding States, solemnly guarantied in the Constitution – recognised by the whole action of the Legislative and Executive departments of the Government from its organization; and sanctioned by repeated decisions of the Supreme Court – rights of person and of property, indispensable to their welfare and happiness.

It is perfectly plain that the attempt to carry out this policy would have been a revolution of the Government by the prostration of the Constitution; and since all efforts on the part of the Southern States to prevent this course were spurned and positively rejected, it was too clear to admit of doubt that the policy was to be pressed to its most oppressive and degrading consummation.

It was, therefore, just and proper that the Southern States should act upon the belief that Mr. Lincoln and his party would carry out the threats and pledges which brought them into power, and which, when called upon, they had solemnly refused to disavow; and it was wise that they should withdraw from the Union before he came into office, if they thought fit to do so.

How well founded these anticipations were, was not long left in doubt after his installation.

Determined to employ all the power of the Government to coerce the seceded States into submission to his authority, but yet dreading to take the initiative in that crusade, the policy was conceived of throwing the responsibility of striking the first blow in the war upon the South. This was to be done by keeping possession of certain forts held by the United States within the limits of the seceded States, so as to compel those States either to acquiesce in their occupation and thereby acknowledge the authority of the United States, or to take them by arms, and incur the responsibility of commencing hostilities. Well knowing that the latter alternative would arise in case they continued to claim and hold these forts, they resorted to this trick as a color for saying, that *the war had been forced upon them* by the arms of the seceded States, and to escape the odium of waging war upon the States – a transparent subterfuge, the fit sequel to the perfidy which constrained the South to resort to force; since the armed occupation of the territory of a seceded State was itself an act of war. It was after the old precedent of the wolf complaining of the lamb, who was drinking at the brook below him, for disturbing the water which the wolf was drinking in the stream above. But it answered the purpose of Mr. Lincoln's Government, and served as a pretext for clamor to enable him to inflame the public feeling and to summon his troops to the field to commence the work of invasion and subjugation against what he believed to be a weak and powerless people.

In violation of solemn and repeated pledges that Fort Sumter should be evacuated, he refused to comply with the pledge, and compelled the Confederate Government to take it by force. Under the pretext of this provocation, he issued his proclamation calling for seventy-five thousand men to invade the seceded States – a palpable usurpation of power, without color of authority under the Constitution or laws of the United States, which aroused Virginia, North Carolina, Tennessee and Arkansas from their lethargy, and compelled them, for the protection of their rights and honor, to follow the course of the seven preceding States, and to secede.

This first act of the Government of Mr. Lincoln has been rapidly followed up by the most startling usurpations of power. It is not the purpose of these remarks to enumerate these outrages, or to dwell upon their enormity. Only the most solemn and deliberately perpetrated of them will be referred to, as showing that the fulfilment has far exceeded the wildest apprehensions of the friends of American institutions, and that the renowned American Union has been transformed into a despotism, the most abject and degraded.

1. The right of personal liberty, guaranteed by

the Constitution, and *placed by it beyond the touch of any or all of the departments of the Government,* is struck down – *a private citizen* of the State of Maryland, *without process* and *without notice of the charge against him,* is seized by military authority, for an alleged civil offense, and hurried to confinement in a fortress of the United States, in violation of the 5th and 6th amended Articles of the Constitution. This case of Merryman has been followed by numberless others of the same character, where citizens of States not seceded, have been immured in fortresses of the United States for more than a year, deprived of the comforts of life, and to the great peril of their health and even their lives from disease and confinement – *without warrant* – *without legal notice of the charges against them* – and all this time denied their constitutional right to be proceeded against by indictment or presentment, to be confronted with the witnesses against them, and to have a speedy trial – rights given to them by amended Articles five and six of the Constitution.

2. Upon the writ of *Habeas Corpus* granted by the Chief Justice of the United States, in the case of Merryman, the party imprisoned was refused to be brought before that Judge, under orders from Mr. Lincoln's Government, claiming and exercising the right to suspend the writ of *Habeas Corpus;* thereby usurping the power given to Congress alone by the Constitution. And this usurpation was persisted in and practiced after the decision of the Chief Justice, that the power assumed by the Government was ille-

gal and a violation of the Constitution. It may safely be said that no King of England could have dared to commit these acts, under any circumstances, without the loss of his head.

3. He struck down the right of freedom of speech and of personal liberty at one blow, in seizing and committing to his Bastiles numerous private citizens of the State of Maryland, and of other States, still members of the Union; whose only offense was the exercise of the right of an American citizen – never questioned since the date of the unconstitutional sedition law of 1798 – to declare their opposition to the unconstitutional acts of Mr. Lincoln, and in peaceably discussing them. He has suppressed many newspaper presses in various parts of the States still continuing in the Union, and committed their editors to prison in distant forts – and all this in flagrant violation of the prohibitions of the first Amendment to the Constitution, denying such powers even to Congress.

4. By armed soldiery, he prevented the assemblage of the Legislature of Maryland according to her Constitution and laws – seized a large number of its members and committed them to close and uncomfortable imprisonment in distant forts, and dispersed the residue by force – thereby suppressing the regular legislative authority of the State, then fully in the Union; because he feared that the Legislature would declare their opposition to his usurpations and take steps to protect the rights of the people of the State against his oppressions; an outrage upon free govern-

ment without a parallel in the history of governments claiming to be free.

5. By his armed soldiers, he seized at the hour of midnight and dragged from their beds and families, without process and without notice of any offense, the Mayor, Marshal and Commissioners of Police of the city of Baltimore, quiet, unoffending citizens of high character, upon no other ground than that they would not yield obedience to his edicts in derogation of their rightful authority under the Constitution and laws of the State, and because they were suspected of being opposed to his unconstitutional acts – thus deposing the regular municipal authority of the city. And these officers have been imprisoned *in a distant fortress, for about eighteen months; without legal notice of the nature and cause of accusation against them; without indictment or presentment; denied of their right to have a speedy trial by a jury of the State where the offense is pretended to have been committed* – sacred rights, positively guarantied by the Fifth and Sixth Amendments to the Constitution. These outrages find their parallel only in the vilest acts of the Jacobins of 1793.

6. "The State Governments are constituent and *essential* parts of the Federal Government," says Mr. Madison in *Federalist*, No. 45.

But the armed forces of Mr. Lincoln, under his authority, have driven the duly constituted State officers from the seats of Government of several of the Southern States, thereby deposing the regular State Governments elected by the people, which, in legal effect, is an abdication of the authority of the United States, since it necessarily excludes such States from the Union. And not content with this act of suicide to the Union, as to those States, he *has appointed Governors for them, and surrounded them with armed forces to suppress the laws of the State, and to execute over the people laws of his own dictation, at the will of his military commanders,* in utter violation of the rights of person and of property of the citizens under the Constitution and laws of the State, recognised and guaranteed by the Constitution of the United States.

He has committed the same outrage upon all justice and right, in deposing the municipal authorities of cities overrun by his forces, setting aside the laws governing them, and superseding them by officers elected under military duress by his own subjects, in violation of the Constitution and of their charters.

7. He has violated the liberty of conscience and desecrated the sanctuaries of God, by disturbing worshipping assemblies in churches, seizing clergymen in the performance of their sacred functions, imprisoning them in jails, penitentiaries and distant forts because they would not offer prayers to the Almighty for the success and prosperity of the Government engaged in the work of invading and plundering the Southern States, and murdering their people – thus violating the First and Fifth Amendments to the Constitution.

8. He has seized and attempted to confiscate

the property of private citizens in the Southern States, not bearing arms, nor indicted or convicted of any crime against the United States, in violation of the Constitution. Claiming that these States are still members of the Union, he has yet waged a war of rapine and destruction against the property of their people indiscriminately, whether belonging to those chargeable with acts of resistance to his Government, or not. He has seduced slaves from their masters and placed arms in their hands, enabling them to commit murder and plunder, and has enlisted many of them as soldiers in his armies. With fire and sword, he has laid waste whole sections of country, regardless of age, sex or condition, in violation alike of the feelings of humanity, and of the laws of civilized war; and now claims whenever he has the power, to strip our people of all their substance, and to deprive them of all their rights under the Constitution – thus rendering it impossible to restore to the Union those States, except their people are disfranchised, degraded and stripped of all property; the necessary effect of which would be either to desolate these States, or to fill them with an imported people, their proper citizens being degraded, stripped of every right of person and of property, and under the ban of imported masters or perhaps of their own slaves. His Government stands forth the enemy alike of the Union, and of the human race.

9. His Government has admitted into the Senate of the United States persons appointed as Senators by a usurped Government of a part of the State

of Virginia, formed in palpable violation of the Constitution and laws of that State, against the right of the regularly elected and constituted governmental departments of that State, then in office and confessedly the legitimate authorities of the State, under her constitution and laws – thereby not only sanctioning a flagrant rebellion and usurpation, but virtually *"forming a new State within the jurisdiction of another State, without the consent of the Legislature"* of that State – in violation of the prohibition of the third section of the fourth Article of the Constitution of the United States.

10. He has usurped the power to declare martial law, by his proclamation of September, 1862. In violation of the positive prohibitions of the Fifth Amended Article of the Constitution – "that no person shall be held to answer for a capital or otherwise infamous crime, unless on a presentment or indictment of a grand jury, except in cases arising in the land and naval forces, or in the militia, when in actual service in time of war or public danger" – he has ordained, that *all persons* discouraging volunteer enlistments, resisting militia drafts, *or guilty of any disloyal practice,* affording aid and comfort to the rebels against the authority of the United States, *shall be subject to martial law, and liable to trial and punishment by court martial or military commission.*

Now the Constitution expressly prohibits any person not belonging to "the land or naval forces or the militia," &c., to be held to answer for any crime *unless on a presentment or indictment of a grand jury.* All the combined departments of the Federal Government had no power to subject such persons to trial in any other mode. And yet this sacred and venerated right is struck down by the edict of Abraham Lincoln; and the private citizen is subjected to the extraordinary proceeding of a court martial or "military commission," to be appointed by the powers which send forth this edict; deprived of the right of trial by jury in the State where the alleged offense was committed; of being confronted by the witnesses against him; of process to compel the attendance of witnesses in his behalf (rights also positively secured to him by the Sixth Amendment of the Constitution); deprived of the process of appeal or writ of error to the Court provided by the Constitution to determine his rights and to settle whether the edict under which he is impaled is valid and constitutional. The annals of usurpation and tyranny in modern times may be searched in vain for the parallel of this reckless and wicked outrage upon a sacred and firmly guarantied right of the citizen, and upon the prohibitions of the Constitution which he had sworn to support. Nothing could exceed it but the tortures of the Inquisition.

  11. The last act that will be here referred to, is the Proclamation declaring that after the first of January, 1863, all slaves within any State whose people shall be in rebellion against the United States shall be forever free; and that *the Executive Government of the United States, naval and military, will maintain their freedom, and will do no act to repress*

them in any efforts they may make for their freedom. This edict, if effectual for the object intended, would at once annihilate a large part of the property of the people composing the Southern States, the right to which is expressly recognised by the Constitution. It would annihilate with it the main business, pursuits, property, wealth and social institutions dependant on that species of property in those States and reduce their people to ruin and their country to desolation. It would raise a servile war of extermination either of the White, or of the slave, population, producing scenes, which no mind but that of a fiend in human form can contemplate without the deepest horror. Yet this vile and flagitious manifesto regards these scenes with encouragement, and promises to "maintain the freedom of such slaves" by the whole power of the Government, and to "do no act to repress them in *any* efforts they may make for freedom." After inciting them to these horrors, their authors are to do no act to repress them in their efforts for freedom, however revolting to humanity! Well may this atrocious act call forth, as it has done, the execrations of the civilized world against the monster who has proclaimed it.

But its gross usurpation and base purpose are not more striking than its shameless violation of the declarations that Mr. Lincoln has made from the date of his inauguration to the time of his proclamation in relation to interfering with slavery in the States. In his inaugural address, he says:

"I have no purpose directly or indirectly to in-

terfere with the institution of slavery in the States. I believe I have no right to do so, and I have no inclination to do so."

In the interview held by him with certain border State members of Congress, on the 10th March, 1862, relative to his proposition to emancipate the slaves on their receiving compensation from the Federal Government, he says:

"That emancipation was a subject exclusively under the control of the States, and must be adopted or rejected by each for itself – that *he did not claim, nor had this Government any right to coerce them for that purpose*" – Mr. Menzies, of Kentucky, enquired "if the President thought there was any power, except in the States themselves, to carry out this scheme of emancipation. The President replied *he thought there could not be."*

In an interview with an embassy of clergymen from Chicago, shortly before the date of this proclamation, he declared that the emancipation of slaves in the States was impracticable, wild and inexpedient, and expressed his determination not to attempt it.

In his veto to the Confiscation and Emancipation bill in July 1862, he says, *"It is startling to say that Congress can free a slave within a State."* If the Legislative department of the Government could not do the act, how much more startling is it that the Executive should usurp so tremendous a power? Yet, notwithstanding all this, this act is but the fulfilment of the pledges and principles which caused his election.

Thus it appears that the Constitution of the United States has been completely set at naught, and the most despotic powers usurped by those holding the Government, not only without authority granted, but in violation of positive prohibitions; and *in most of these acts, the usurpation stands confessed by its authors.* If there was virtue enough in Congress to impeach him for usurpation, he could be convicted by his own recorded admissions of wilful violations of his oath to support the Constitution, in repeated instances.

And now what is the justification or palliation for these high crimes? It is the old plea of tyrants – *necessity* – that the powers conferred upon the Government by the Constitution were insufficient to suppress the alleged rebellion; consisting in the withdrawal of eleven sovereign States, in the most solemn form known to political action, and with great and acknowledged unanimity, from a Union which was to be perverted to the destruction of all their rights under the Constitution, and in forming a new and independent government of their own choice among themselves; not, in any wise, interfering with the rights of the remaining States – and, therefore, that it was necessary for the Government of the remaining United States to violate the Constitution and assume the powers of a dictatorship, in order to preserve the Constitution and to restore the dismembered Union!

If such a necessity could exist, it would seem to furnish the most unanswerable reason why the Government could not make war upon the seceded

States without converting itself into a despotism. For it would be the height of absurdity and wickedness to attempt to restore the Union by war against the seceded States, when this plea of necessity confesses that, in order to make the effort successful, it was necessary to destroy their State and municipal governments; to rob the people of all their property; to deprive them of all their rights under their State governments; in fact, to annihilate their political existence, as the people of the States, and to render it impossible to restore the Union with the rights and privileges of the States preserved; and to do all this by the prostration of the most solemn guaranties of the Constitution.

But it is preposterous to say that the Union, which rests solely on the Constitution, can be preserved by violating the fundamental principles of that Great Charter of the Union. The idea is stupidly and insultingly absurd, that any necessity can justify the violation of the law of its existence in order to maintain its existence. As well might we talk of undermining a foundation for the purpose of preserving its superstructure; or of a man's stabbing himself to the heart, to preserve his constitution. The disguise is too transparent to deceive any but those who wickedly shut their eyes to the truth.

It is the will, and not any proper necessity, that has produced these acts. It is the death struggle for the consummation of the long-foreshadowed and long-deferred hopes of power and plunder to be visited upon the South, rendered desperate by the fear that these sordid schemes were, at last, about to be disappointed and blasted forever, when fruition seemed to be within their very grasp; it is the necessity for the perpetration of the unholy ends of avarice and abolitionism against the South, which were thwarted by her withdrawal beyond the power of her oppressors: these are the causes which have brought to light this profound love for the Union, and this amazing devotion to the Constitution!

And now the astounding development stands forth from the grand *oriflamme* of Abolitionism at Washington – that the Southern States were not to be allowed to enjoy their solemnly guaranteed rights *in the Union,* nor suffered to enjoy them by withdrawing *from the Union* –

That it was settled that property in slaves was to be abolished if the Southern States had remained in the Union; but since they have been compelled to withdraw from the Union to protect their rights, slavery is now to be abolished, *because they seceded:* and thus the necessity which the wrong of the oppressors forced upon them is made the justification for the outrage intended against them from the first, and now boldly proclaimed –

That the people of these States must either submit, in the Union, to be robbed of all their most sacred rights secured by the Constitution, or be visited, if they withdraw from the Union, with fire and sword, with plunder and murder, their own slaves armed and incited to the most horrid deeds of destruction and brutality against all ages, sexes and conditions of the White race, because these people were driven, for the necessary protection of their dearest rights, to withdraw from the grasp of the usurper and tyrant –

That the people of these States are to be deprived of every right, and despoiled of all their substance, reduced to penury and degradation, with imported masters from the hordes of their enemies to seize their property, with Vandal rapacity, under despotic edicts, and to control the public acts and destinies of these States; thereby at once annihilating all the rights of persons and of property in these States, destroying the State governments, and reducing them to dependencies of the despotism which grinds them under its iron heel – and all this in the name of the Union, and for the sake of the Constitution!

These designs, at first disguised, now stand out in all their horrors, openly avowed under the pretext of necessity; and now the contest waged by Abraham Lincoln against the Confederate States, exhibits an open and undisguised struggle between Constitutional government, civil and religious liberty, good faith and justice, on the one side; and tyranny, fanaticism, robbery and Red Republicanism, on the other. In such a contest, surely the South had no course but resistance to the oppressions by all the means which God and nature have placed in her hands.

Nero set fire to the ancient edifices of Rome, as unsuited to his times and taste, destroying those monuments of her antiquity and grandeur, together with the memorials of her victories, in a common conflagration; and Abraham Lincoln has laid his impious hand upon the Constitution, the bulwark of our liberties and the chief monument of our national glory, as unsuited to his political ideas and unfit for the purposes of his myrmidons. It must overwhelm the heart of every true American patriot with unutterable shame and sorrow, that such should be the end of the once glorious Union erected by the patriots and sages of the Revolution – reduced to ruin by profligate men, incapable of good, yet potent for evil, in tearing down the pillars which supported the noble structure; and that all that now remains of it is a miserable wreck – the terror of its adherents and the scorn of its enemies; the scourge of this country and the contempt of the civilized world.

October, 1862.

APPENDIX ONE
Speech Delivered by Hon. A. H. Handy in the City of Baltimore, Maryland on December 19th, 1860[1]

Hon. A.H. Handy, a native Marylander, who had located in Mississippi, was accredited by the Governor of that State to call on the Governor of Maryland, in advocacy of concerted action between all the Southern States. Governor Hicks declined to receive him. Mr. Handy visited Baltimore, and on the night of December 19th, 1860, delivered an address to fifteen hundred people in the Maryland Institute. On the rostrum were Zenas Barnum, Beal H. Richardson, William G. Harrison, George W. Herring, William D. Hughes, William H. Purnell, William Nelson and Coleman Yellott. Mr. Harrison pre-

---

1. Extracted from Henry E. Shepherd, ed., *History of Baltimore, Maryland, 1729-1898* (Uniontown, Pennsylvania: S.B. Nelson, 1898), pp. 129ff.

sided. Mr. Handy was received with three cheers. The purport of his speech was "that he had been appointed by the State of Mississippi a commissioner to the State of Maryland to counsel with the authorities in the present crisis, not for the purpose of rousing or exciting the feeling of the Marylanders upon the great questions pending. His father and grandfather were Marylanders and he was born upon her soil. He wished to secure the co-operation of Maryland and Mississippi to defend those sacred institutions left by the fathers to the people of the South. Mississippi, as heretofore, was for the preservation of the Union and the maintenance of the Constitution. If any man said that Mississippi is disloyal, that man he would brand a libeller. Should Mr. Lincoln be elected the institutions of the South would be prostituted and subverted. In Mississippi the people believed that the institution of slavery was ordained by God and sanctioned by humanity.

"It was an institution ordained for the amelioration of the condition of the slave, and there is a moral duty imposed upon the slave-holder to protect his slave. Those at the North say slavery is forbidden by God, is not sanctioned by humanity, and that slaves cannot be held without sin. These ideas have long been entertained and instilled into the Northern mind until they now believe such teachings to be the truth. They have agitated the subject and denounced the institution until the country is shrouded in gloom. Commerce and every source of prosperity has been submerged by the 'irrepressible conflict,' which has determined that all States must either be free or slave. The South cannot do without slavery; the cotton and other interests will not admit of it, and we do not intend to be without it.

"The project of the North is first to abolish slavery in all the new territories, at the military posts and in the District of Columbia. Thus slavery would be confined to the States where it now exists, and in a few years would be excluded altogether, because the new States to be admitted as free will have such a preponderance, that they will overpower and crush out the last vestige of slavery.

"Mr. Lincoln's position is, that slavery shall be kept where it now is, and no one will be permitted to travel beyond the limits of his own State with his slaves. We have as much right to sell them as we have to sell our horses and cows, or any other property. Another movement to be inaugurated in Congress was, that Northerners shall be permitted to express their abolition views in Southern States – to send incendiary publications throughout those States, calculated to incite insurrection and cause the slaves to cut the throats of their masters.

"It is not their intention to interfere with slavery where it exists, but they intend to excite the minds of the slaves and make them so much dreaded that the States holding them will be forced for their own safety to set them free. Abraham Lincoln would have postmasters and other officers throughout the South, to facilitate the circulation of those incendiary documents, and thus encourage slaves to rise and kill their masters.

"It is argued on the other hand that Lincoln has yet done no overt act, and that it is to be hoped he will not perform any act contrary to the Constitution. That he will not dare to carry them out. Let me tell you that Abraham Lincoln is a brave and self-willed man, and will not betray the parties that elected him upon those pledges. We have his promise and pledge made when a member of Congress, and when he ran against Mr. Douglas in Illinois, that he will do so, and his acts will be violations of our rights.

"They have trampled under foot the Constitution by passing laws nullifying its provisions with regard to slavery, and we can but expect that he as their representative will carry them out when in the Presidential chair. The election of Abraham Lincoln is a violation of the Constitution, and shall we wait until he acts? [Cries of "No."] Men are already elected to execute their laws of oppression upon you, and will you submit? [Cries of "No," "No."] Mr. Lincoln is approaching with the sword of office in his hands, and when he gets in, you may rest assured he will act. We have expostulated, prayed and beseeched those people to recognize and accord us our rights, but they have scorned and spoken of it only as Southern thunder. We of Mississippi are of one opinion that these things cannot longer be endured. We must now stand upon and demand our rights.

"It is said that Congress has power to settle the question. Why, they have appointed a committee of thirty-three, and they are now busily engaged in doing nothing. This committee consists chiefly of Northerners. One of them is from your State." [Hisses.] Referring to Henry Winter Davis.

A scene of wild excitement ensued, several persons who had been intently listening to the speaker rose from their seats and cheered for Henry Winter Davis, others responded in hisses, some one crying out, "Oh! he is a black Republican." Cheers rang out for Bell all over the hall, and there was counter-cheering for Breckenridge, mingled with cries of "put him out." After further cheering and hissing the disturbance calmed down.

Mr. Handy, proceeding, said: "This is no party matter; every son of the South was deeply interested in it. Some of the warmest advocates of Mississippi's course were friends of Mr. Bell. This committee for the most part were black Republicans, and will never recognize slavery as a Constitutional right. Just put the question to them: Do you recognize slavery as a Constitutional right? and they will explode immediately. There is nothing to be expected from them except a delay that will ruin the country. The fugitive slave law has been disregarded and set aside. They won't believe in it, and if they won't believe in Moses and the prophets, they won't believe in any one, though he comes from the dead.

"Mississippi was opposed to calling a convention of all the slave-holding States. There is not time for it between this and the 4th of March. Legislatures would have to be called together, and this could not be done in season. Maryland and Texas have difficulties in the way of an immediate convening of their Legislatures. But suppose the convention was called, was there any probability that they would agree before the 4th of March? Not at all. It would take longer time to deliberate. But there was a still stronger objection. It was contrary to the Constitution.

"It would be a meeting of the States held in the Union to deliberate on the dissolution of the Union. This they cannot do. If the Union is to be broken up, each State must act in her sovereign capacity. They must go out of the Union one by one as they came into it. We of Mississippi do not see that there is to be anything gained by a convention of all the Southern States. Our views, as I present them for your consideration, are that each Southern State shall secede from the Union."

At this point further disorder transpired. There were hissings and cheerings and cries of "put the black Republicans out." Then followed cheers for the Union; cheers for Governor Hicks; cheers for South Carolina, and hisses.

The speaker resumed when the confusion died out, saying, "he was not there to arouse their passions. He was in his native State to speak the truth and he could not be deterred by hisses. If the views he presented were not sound ones, reject them. We have tried all expedients to secure our rights which the wits of man could devise, but have failed. We do not take this step for the purpose of breaking up the Union, but to have our rights guaranteed.

"Our fathers fought to make these States free and sovereign, and afterwards agreed to enter into a compact with the other States. This is the contract that has been trampled upon. We want our rights under the Constitution and we are determined to have them out of the Union if we cannot have them in. It is said the Constitution has nothing in it giving a State power to secede. This is true. It has nothing in it giving you the power to have a legislature or municipal government in your city, but all powers not given to the General Government and enumerated in the Constitution were reserved to the States, and they have the power to resume their sovereign rights whenever they shall see fit to do so.

"Suppose, for example, that the State of Maryland, for the preservation of her rights, should withdraw from the Union; would not the act of coercion to bring her back make her subjugated and disgraced, and not equal to the rest of the States by reason of her subjugation. Therefore, the act of coercion is, in itself, the destruction of the Union, because it destroys the equality of the States. Permit me to say something upon secession. We do not propose to go out of the Union for the purpose of breaking up the Union. We go out for the purpose of getting our rights in the Union. The withdrawing is to have amendments made by the Northern States, so that we may have guaranteed us our rights forever. We only want our rights protected, and we want the guarantee that they shall not again be trampled upon. We want them now and forever. If the question is not settled now and finally we will go out and form a provincial government, and wait until it is settled, and then come back. If it is never settled we will stay out. We want no new laws; we are satisfied with the Constitution and the Supreme Court, but we want those laws we have fully and faithfully enforced. This is the position of Mississippi, and I think it is the position of Maryland.

"If the Southern States are severed from the Northern States – which I hope may not be the case – it will be as the amputation of an arm to save the body. He would not advise Maryland, but before Mr. Lincoln comes into power Mississippi will be out of the Union. We do not intend that Lincoln and his myrmidons shall have power and dominion over us, unless such amendments are made to the Constitution as will settle the question forever. It has been said that if the South secedes she will be overrun by troops. For this we are prepared, as is also South Carolina, and if Northern men are disposed to make a raid upon us like the John Brown raid or any other, we will say to them come on. But before they do so we would advise them to contemplate the bravery of South Carolina troops at Cherubusco, and of the Mississippians at Monterey and Buena Vista, and then try to imagine how the sons of the South will stand when their homes are besieged and the lives of their wives, daughters and sisters are at stake."

APPENDIX TWO
Governor's Message[1]

Executive Office, Jackson Mississippi
November 26th, 1860

Gentlemen of the Senate and House of Representatives:

It is with deep regret that I am constrained to forego the usual congratulations for peace, prosperity, and bright hopes for the future, which have formed so marked a feature of Executive Communications to the Legislative Departments of the sovereign States of this once happy Confederacy. In performance of what I deemed an imperative duty, I have convened in extraordinary session, to take into consideration the greatest and most solemn question that ever engaged the attention of any Legislative body on this Continent. One involving more human

---

1. *Journal of the Senate of the State of Mississippi* (Jackson: E. Barksdale, State Printer, 1860), pp. 5ff.

happiness or human misery than any political question of the age in which we live. On the solution of which hangs the destiny, for weal or woe, not only of this generation and this age, but of all generations which come after us, for an indefinite term of centuries, the end of which no prophet can foretell.

The existence or abolition of African slavery in the Southern States is now up for final settlement before that tribunal which has exclusive jurisdiction – the people of the Southern States where it exists. It is true that the forms of a trial have been had before the people of the non-slave holding States. The institutions of the South have been dragged before that tribunal, in violation of every principle of the Constitution, and of common sense, and tried before a Court having no jurisdiction, and a jury ignorant of the law and the facts; and the verdict thus obtained is, that slavery is sinful and must be destroyed. We are told that this verdict will be executed, that the Northern mind will never rest satisfied until slavery is placed in such a condition as will insure its ultimate extinction, and that all the power the Southern States now have in the final settlement of this matter, is to choose whether it shall be a peaceable and gradual abolition, or speedy and violent. These are the hard terms offered to fifteen States of this Confederacy, as if they were conquered and not co-equal States, as if the superior numbers of the Northern States gave them the constitutional right to regulate the domestic affairs of the Southern States, without consulting their wishes, and against their consent. Submission to such a rule establishes a despotism under which the dearest rights of the Southern States are held at the sufferance of a people ignorant of their wants, and hostile to their rights. If they were honest and just, they are so utterly ignorant of the capacities and necessities of two races which inhabit the Southern section of this Confederacy, as to render it impossible for them to rule it with success or manage it without ruin. It would be as reasonable to expect the steamship to make a successful voyage across the Atlantic with crazy men for engineers, as to hope for a prosperous future for the South under Black Republican rule. Can the lives, liberty and property of the people of Mississippi be safely entrusted to the keeping of that sectional majority which must hereafter administer the Federal Government?

I think they cannot, for the following reasons:

They have exhibited a low selfishness in seizing all the Territories, which are the common property of all the States. They have deliberately attempted to, and have succeeded in educating a generation to hate the South. They have sworn to support the Federal Constitution, and deliberately passed laws with the palpable intent to violate one of the plainest provisions of that compact. They have sent large sums of money to Congress, for the purpose of bribing the members of that body to pass laws to advance their private interests. They have attempted to degrade us in the estimation of other nations, by denouncing us as barbarians, pirates and robbers, unfit associates for Christian or civilized men. They have excited our slaves to insurrection, advised them to burn our property and murder our people, and have furnished them with arms and ammunition to aid them in their bloody work. They have murdered Southern men in the lawful pursuit of their fugitive slaves, and failed to punish their citizens for these flagrant violations of the laws of God and man. They have furnished money and arms for the invasion of a slaveholding State, and when the punishment awarded to treason and murder by all civilized nations, overtook the invaders, they threatened the dastardly revenge of midnight incendiaries, tolled bells in honor of traitors and murderers, and rewarded the family of the chief traitor as never was rewarded that of any soldier who fell in defence of the country, and held him up as an example of heroic devotion to a just and glorious cause. Their Press, Pulpit, Lecture Room and Forum teem daily and nightly with exhortations to their people to press forward this war on our institutions even to the drenching of Southern fields with the blood of her citizens.

In view of all this long catalogue of insults and injuries, in view of the fact that this hostile section must continue to increase in power, I feel that I am warranted in saying that the Northern people have forfeited the confidence of the people of Mississippi, and that the lives, liberty and property of ourselves, and our children after us, ought not to be entrusted to rulers elected by such a people. The judgment of the people of all the Southern States bears me out in this conclusion, for the candidate recently elected to the Presidency, gets not one electoral vote in all the fifteen slave States. While our Northern assailants have only the power of the press, mobs and State governments to aid them in these aggressions, it was the opinion of many of our wisest and best men that we might still defend ourselves in the Union, by the power of our State governments with the aid of the Federal Government. But when, in a recent Presidential election, a large majority have decreed that the Federal Government, with all its immense powers, on which we relied for protection, shall hereafter be administered by the same class of men who have been guilty of all these acts of violence and bad faith, it is folly, it is madness to hope for safety in such a Government. To remain longer but adds weight and power to the arm that strikes us, and takes from us the power of returning the blows. Surveying the whole field, in view of the past history, the present attitude and future probabilities of this great question, I see but one path of honor and safety for Mississippi. Let her say to the Black Republican States as Abraham said to Lot: "Let there be no strife, I pray thee, between me and thee, and between my herdmen and thy herdmen, for we be brethren. Separate thyself, I pray thee, from me, if thou wilt take the left hand then I will go to the right; if thou depart to the right hand then I will go to the left."

That Mississippi may be enabled to speak on this grave subject in her sovereign capacity, I recommend that a Convention be called, to meet at an early day. The State, thus assembled, will have a right to decide for itself the mode and measures of redress, for all violations of the rights of her citizens, or the rights of the State, either by the Northern States, the people of the Northern States, or the Federal Government. That this right does exist in the sovereign States of this Confederacy, is plainly deducible from the history of all the political bodies which originated and organized this system of American Governments. The first great leading idea that lies at the base of our whole system, is found in that clause of the Declaration of Independence which declares:

"We hold these truths to be self-evident, that all men are created equal; that they are endowed by their Creator with certain inalienable rights: that among these, are life, liberty and the pursuit of happiness. That to secure these rights, governments are instituted among men, deriving their just powers from the consent of the governed, that whenever any form of government becomes destructive to these ends, it is the right of the people to alter or abolish it, and to institute a new government, laying its foundation on such principles, and organizing its powers in such form as to them may seem most likely to effect their safety and happiness."

This short sentence contains the parent principle of our system of governments, both State and Federal, and any party which attempts to ignore it in the administration of these Governments, must prepare to meet the spirit of '76. Separate and independent communities, with governments deriving their powers from the consent of the governed, the Colonies commenced the war of the Revolution. Separate and independent communities they declared themselves sovereign and independent States, and entered as such into articles of confederation. In their treaty of peace with Great Britain they were acknowledged to be sovereign and independent States. These sovereign States assembled in convention at Philadelphia on terms of perfect equality, to reorganize their confederation, to form a more perfect Union of sovereign States; and when in that Convention it was proposed to give to the larger States the power to govern – the smaller without their consent, by giving them representation in both branches of the Federal Congress in proportion to their population – the necessity of union growing out of the then feebleness of the States – confidence engendered by seven years of brotherhood in arms, and the presence of Washington himself, would not have saved the Convention from disruption if the larger States had not acknowledged this great and vital principle in the confederation, by giving the smaller States perfect equality in that most important branch of the Federal Congress which has the treaty making power, and the power to negative alike the appointments of the President and the enactments of the House of Representatives. Again, when in that Convention it was proposed to give to the Federal Government the power to "call forth the force of the Union against any member of the Confederacy failing to do its duty under the articles thereof," men of all parties sprang to their feet and denounced it as violative of the rights of the States and dangerous to the liberties of the people, and voted it down unanimously. If any party shall be found reckless enough to attempt to usurp this power for the Federal Government, thus positively denied to it by the Convention, men of all parties will spring to their feet and again vindicate the rights of the States and the liberty of the people.

When this Constitution was finally agreed to in the Convention of Philadelphia, it was submitted to the several States, and each State for itself and by itself, ratified it. Nor was it ordained and established between the people of any State and those of the other States, except by the separate and sovereign act of that State. The Convention of New York declared in their act of ratification, that the powers of the Government may be re-assumed by the people whensoever it shall become necessary to their happiness. What people is here meant? The people of New York! for that Convention could speak for no other. The Convention of the State of Virginia, in her act of ratification, in the name and in behalf of the people of Virginia, declared that "the powers granted under the Constitution, being derived from the people of the United States, may be resumed by them whensoever the same shall be perverted to their injury or oppression." Who, was it feared, might pervert these granted powers to the injury and oppression of the people of Virginia? The majority of the States by their votes in the Congress, and in the election of the President. Could Virginia mean that only a majority of "the people of these United States" had the right to resume the powers granted under the Constitution? This construction would make their declaration idle and senseless, for that same majority could control the action of the Government and prevent the perversion of its powers. That Convention "speaking in the name and in behalf of the people of Virginia," must have intended to declare that the people of Virginia had a right to re-assume the power which they had granted to the Federal Government whenever the same shall be perverted to their injury or oppression, and used the phrase "the people of the United States" to express a double idea, declaring the right of the people of Virginia, and admitting the right of the people of each of the States to resume the powers granted under the Constitution, whenever the same shall be perverted to their injury or oppression. The people of Rhode Island, in her act of ratification, were still more explicit in reserving this right. Her Convention declared in that act, that there are rights of which they could not deprive or divest their posterity, among which they enumerate the right of pursuing and obtaining happiness, possessing and protecting property, and to guard these among others, from the usurpations or abuses of the Federal Government, they declared that "the powers of the Government may be re-assumed by the people, whensoever it shall become necessary to their happiness."

The right to be governed only by their own consent, and to withdraw whenever it is necessary for their safety, are parts of the reserved rights of the States. Those who have arrived at a different conclusion, seem to have ignored the history of the action of the States, and gone to the words of the Constitution to seek there the reserved rights of the States, and when they find in the preamble of that instrument the words, "We, the People of the United States, do ordain and establish this Constitution, for the United States of America," they contend that this Government was ordained and established by the whole people for the States, and over the States, and is consequently binding on the States until the whole people of the United States relieves them of the obligation to obey it. This construction is contradicted alike by the facts of history and the words of the Constitution. History shows that it was made and agreed to by the States, the smaller States an equal voice with the larger States in the adoption of every clause in it, and that it was ratified and established by the States," each acting independently by itself and for itself, and the words of the Constitution in the seventh article are as follows: "The ratification of the Convention of nine States shall be sufficient for the establishment of this Constitution between the States so ratifying the same." Thus the Constitution agreeing with the facts of history shows that it was established by the States and not by the whole people of the United States; and was to be binding between the States that ratified it, and not over them – binding between the States which might ratify, and not between them and States refusing to ratify. For the ratification of twelve States would not and did not make it binding between them and the smallest State of the former Confederacy, Rhode Island, until on her own terms and in her own time, her sovereign act made her one of the States of the new Confederacy.

Again, it is asserted that the supremacy of the Federal Government over the States was established and agreed to in the seventh clause of the sixth article of the Constitution, as follows:

"This Constitution, and the laws of the United States which shall be made in pursuance thereof, and all treaties made, or which shall be made, under the authority of the United States, shall be the supreme law of the land; and the Judges of every State shall be bound thereby, anything in the Constitution or laws of any State to the contrary notwithstanding."

This clause asserts the supremacy of the Constitution, laws and treaties of the Federal Government over the constitutions, laws, courts and citizens of the States so long as they remain united, but does not touch, and was not intended to touch the question of the right of a State to resume this, with the other granted powers, and to cease to be one of the United States. This Constitution, the laws and treaties are declared to be the supreme law of the land. What land? The territories of the States remaining in the Confederacy, and not the territory of the State after it has withdrawn from it. The States did not in this clause of the Constitution, surrender the right which they had so jealously watched over through all stages of its formation.

It thus seems to me clear, that the right to be governed only by their own consent, and to withdraw from the Government for tyranny and oppression is the birth-right of the States, which our fathers guarded for us, never losing sight of it, never surrendering it. And we must guard it for our sons. It is to-day in more imminent peril than at any time since Washington crossed the Delaware. That danger arises from the fact that Mr. Lincoln is to be President for the next four years. That, were it unattended by other threatening circumstances, would be a matter of small moment; but when it is remembered that a struggle has been going on, between the two great sections of the Confederacy, for forty years, the North struggling for domination, for the power to oppress and injure the South, the Southern States defending their existence as equals in the Confederacy, asking nothing but what was given by the Constitution and guaranteed by oaths; and when that dominant, hostile Northern section has attained numbers sufficient to place itself permanently in the ascendant, and add the powers of the Federal Government to its means of oppression, well may we regard this as the great danger, that constrains men of all parties in the South to bury party feuds and band together for defense. Our deliverance from this great danger, in my opinion, is to be found in the reserved right of the States to withdraw from injury and oppression"which was retained by those who formed this Government, for just such an emergency as this. Embodied in the reserved rights of the States, is the soul of American Liberty. The great saving principle to which alone the Southern States can *look and live*. This saving principle must perish under Black Republican rule. Then go down into Egypt while Herod reigns in Judea" it is the only means of saving the life of this Emanuel of American politics. And when, in after years, it shall be told you that they who sought the life of this Prince of Peace and Fraternity are dead, you may come up out of Egypt, and realize all the fond hopes of patriots and sages, of peace on earth and good will among men, under the benign influence of a re-united Government, deriving its just powers from the consent of the governed.

That the State of Mississippi may evince to her Southern sister States the interest she feels in the common danger, I recommend that commissioners be appointed to visit such of them as may convoke their Legislatures or call Conventions to take into consideration the threatening attitude of the Northern States, and the Northern sectional administration about to be inaugurated at Washington; that they may be informed that Mississippi does not intend to submit to that administration, and we may learn in the most authentic form what are their aims and purposes in the premises.

I recommend that an appropriation be made to each volunteer company, of a sum sufficient to pay all reasonable expenses attending encampments, on days appointed for exercise and instruction; keeping their arms and equipments, so that the young men who give their time and undergo the labor of preparing themselves as soldiers to defend the rights of the States may not be required to expend one dollar of their private means. I recommend that a coat of arms be adopted for the State of Mississippi. In view of the unsettled condition of our political affairs, and the probable great derangement of monetary and commercial relations of the country, and to prevent the ruinous sacrifice of the property of the people of this State, I recommend that an act be passed staying the bringing of suits and the collection of debts by execution sales, until the close of the next regular session of the Legislature.

As it is more than probable that many of the citizens of the border States, may seek a market for their slaves in the cotton States, I recommend the passage of an act prohibiting the introduction of slaves into this State, unless their owners come with them and become citizens, and the introduction of slaves for sale by all persons, whomsoever.

Permit me, in conclusion, again to refer to the great danger to the State which has brought you from your homes, and to exhort my countrymen not to be "caught by the fatal bait of temporary ease and quiet," not to submit to great, disgraceful and certain evils, from a dread of others which may prove to be imaginary. If we falter now, we and our sons must pay the penalty in future years, of bloody, if not fruitless efforts to retrieve the fallen fortunes of the State, which if finally unsuccessful must leave our fair land blighted – cursed with Black Republican politics and free negro morals, to become a cesspool of vice, crime, and infamy.

Can we hesitate! when one bold resolve, bravely executed, makes the aggressor, one united effort makes safe our homes? May the God of our fathers put it into the hearts of the people to make it.

John H. Pettus

APPENDIX THREE
A Declaration of the Immediate Causes Which Induce and Justify the Secession of the State of Mississippi From the Federal Union[1]

In the momentous step which our State has taken of dissolving its connection with the government of which we so long formed a part, it is but just that we should declare the prominent reasons which have induced our course.

Our position is thoroughly identified with the institution of slavery – the greatest material interest of the world. Its labor supplies the product which constitutes by far the largest and most important portions of the commerce of the earth. These products are peculiar to the climate verging on the tropical regions, and by an imperious law of nature, none but the black race can bear exposure to the tropical

---

[1]. Adopted by the State convention meeting in Jackson from January 7-26, 1861.

sun. These products have become necessities of the world, and a blow at slavery, is a blow at commerce and civilization. That blow has long been aimed at the institution, and was at the point of reaching its consummation. There was no choice left us but submission to the mandates of abolition, or a dissolution of the Union, whose principles had been subverted to work out our ruin.

That we do not overstate the dangers to our institution, a reference to a few facts will sufficiently prove.

The hostility to this institution commenced before the adoption of the Constitution, and was manifested in the well-known Ordinance of 1787, in regard to the North-western territory.

The feeling increased, until, in 1819-20, it deprived the South of more than half the vast territory acquired from France.

The same hostility dismembered Texas, and seized upon all the territory acquired from Mexico.

It has grown until it denies the right of property in slaves, and refuses protection to that right on the high seas, in the territories, and whenever the government of the United States had jurisdiction.

It refuses the admission of new slave States into the Union, and seeks to extinguish it by confining it within its present limits, denying the power of expansion.

It tramples the original equality of the South under foot.

It has nullified the Fugitive Slave Law in almost every free State in the Union, and has utterly broken the compact which our fathers pledged their faith to maintain.

It advocates negro equality, socially and politically, and promotes insurrection and incendiarism in our midst.

It has enlisted the press, its pulpit and its schools against us, until the whole popular mind of the North is excited and inflamed with prejudice.

It has made combinations and formed associations to carry out its schemes of emancipation in the States and wherever else slavery exists.

It seeks not to elevate or to support the slave, but to destroy his present condition without providing a better.

It has invaded a State, and invested with the honors of martyrdom, the wretch whose purpose was to apply flames to our dwellings, and the weapons of destruction to our lives.

It has broken every compact into which it has entered for our security.

It has given indubitable evidence of its design to ruin our agriculture, to prostrate our industrial pursuits, and to destroy our social system.

It knows no relenting or hesitation in its purposes; it stops not in its march of aggression, and leaves us no room to hope for cessation or for pause.

It has recently obtained control of the Government, by the prosecution of its unhallowed schemes, and destroyed the last expectation of living together in friendship and brotherhood.

Utter subjugation awaits us in the Union, if we should consent longer to remain in it. It is not a matter of choice, but of necessity. We must either submit to degradation, and to the loss or property worth four billions of money, or we must secede from the Union framed by our fathers, to secure this as well as every other species of property. For far less cause than this, our fathers separated from the Crown of England.

Our decision is made. We follow their footsteps. We embrace the alternative of separation; and for the reasons here stated, we resolve to maintain our rights with the full consciousness of the justice of our course, and the undoubting belief of our ability to maintain it.

APPENDIX FOUR
The Secession of Mississippi[1]

At no time in the history of Mississippi has the State been more ably represented in Congress than the few years preceding her secession, 1858-60. Men with conservative minds like those of L. Q. C. Lamar, Reuben Davis, William Barksdale, Otho Singleton, John A. Quitman, representatives of the Lower House of Congress, the powerful and fluent-tongued speakers like A. G. Brown and Jefferson Davis in the Upper House, are seldom found at one time in the legislative hall representing one sovereign State.

As we scan the records of these men, we read the history of the people who composed our State and understand, without any great power of interpretation, the tense feelings permeating the entire body

---

1. Essay by Mrs. J.E. Brown, historian, Mississippi Division, United Daughters of the Confederacy; *The Confederate Veteran*, Vol. XXXIX:2 (February, 1931), pp. 92ff.

politic at that time, and which existed in the hearts of every citizen relative to the protection of his own property and the State's rights. These men with their master minds were able to answer any and all questions pertaining to the important issues impending in Congress. They injected into their discussions only the highest principles of right and justice, gathered from careful research and after serious investigation. In fact, they were able to meet every attack upon our great government made by Northern propagandists.

On the eleventh of October, 1858, Jefferson Davis delivered his celebrated speech before the Democracy of Boston, Mass., reaffirming the doctrine of State sovereignty, eliciting the highest praise throughout the South, yet creating a furor throughout the nation. In the 36th Congress of 1859, Davis submitted to the Senate a series of resolutions on important issues involving Southern rights, all of them passing the Senate by a large majority.

Let us not forget that, in 1850, Mississippi leaders had called a meeting of delegates from Southern States to be held at Nashville, Tenn. This was the first meeting of its kind held in the South, and matters pertaining to the States were discussed. This leadership in State affairs gave the Mississippi delegation a great deal of prestige when the Democratic National Convention convened, April 23, 1860, at Charleston, S. C. Refusing to adopt the platform instituted by the Northwestern Democrats, our delegates, with those of Alabama, Florida, and Texas, withdrew from the convention. This action helped to create a sentiment which defeated the purpose of the convention. The remaining delegates failed to decide upon a candidate for nomination. The convention adjourned to meet in Baltimore, June 18.

Jefferson Davis had not approved of the delegation seceding from the convention, because he knew that a more solid and enduring triumph could be achieved by remaining together and defeating Douglas. In a tactful way, Davis influenced the return of Mississippi delegates to Baltimore. At the Baltimore convention, however, the Mississippi and the South Carolina delegations refused to participate because all of the seceding States were not admitted to the convention. Douglas was nominated by the remaining delegates, and this split the Democratic party, a most lamentable fact.

The seceding delegates called another meeting later at Richmond and in June nominated John C. Breckinridge for President. The campaign was a most bitter struggle, and, as a result of this contention, Lincoln was elected to the Presidency of the United States of America by a majority of electoral votes only.

In Mississippi only a small party of Foote Democrats, or Constitutional Unionists, had opposed the action of our delegates. The State of Mississippi was not, therefore, so seriously divided upon political issues. The election of John J. Pettus to the executive office in Mississippi followed the presidential election, and this particular selection of governor gave Mississippi liberty to voice the utterances of our foremost leaders. In his message to the State legislature, Governor Pettus counseled a separation, peaceably, if possible, between the Northern and Southern States, but separation nevertheless. He enumerated the grievances of the South and upbraided the North for its sectional views as opposed to the Constitution of the United States of America. He invited a meeting of the Congressional representatives to a conference in Jackson, to consider immediate steps for secession. At this meeting Governor Pettus presented a telegram from South Carolina asking advice as to whether the ordinance of secession then before the legislature should take effect immediately or upon the fourth of March. The majority of our representatives voted "immediately." The governor of South Carolina was duly notified.

Our legislature, in session in November, 1860, passed the bill recommended by Governor Pettus, providing for an election of county delegates, December 29, to a State convention to be held in Jackson, January 7. "The purpose of this convention, or meeting, is to discuss the relations of the U.S.A. to the citizens of Mississippi, and to adopt measures vindicating the sovereignty of the State." The action of other States was not to be considered. We were to discuss our own grievances and the protection of our own institutions. On December 20, 1860, the day set aside for our election, the State of South Carolina passed an ordinance of secession.

The delegates chosen at our regular election met in Jackson on the day designated. This historic body met in the Hall of Representatives and was called together and to order by Samuel Gholson, a leading citizen and an attorney at law. William S. Barry, of Lowndes County, was elected President. Two distinct classes of delegates were present. One faction was for unconditional secession. The other faction was favorable to secession, conditioned upon the border States acquiescing in the act of secession. On the morning of January 9, 1861, Mr. Lamar reported to the convention, then in session, a resolution prepared by a committee of fifteen delegates. This resolution read as follows: "An ordinance to dissolve the Union between the State of Mississippi and other States united with her under the compact entitled 'The Constitution of the United States of America.'" In the afternoon of this same day the ordinance was submitted to the body then in open session and was adopted by a vote of 84 to 15. James L. Alcorn, a leader of one faction rather opposed to the ordinance, voted with the ayes. When his name was called, he arose and said: "Mr. President, the die is cast, the Rubicon is crossed. I follow the army that goes to Rome. I vote for the ordinance." Mr. Brook, another of the leading Whigs, responded in a manner similar to that of Alcorn. In fact, those who had opposed immediate secession joined in with the majority after the first ballot was taken. It was a very solemn occasion, and when the voice of Rev. Whitfield Harrington was heard invoking divine blessing and guidance, tears were in the eyes of some, while the whole audience of spectators, delegates, and officials bowed their heads in reverence. Mrs. Dunbar Rowland, of Mississippi, in *The Heart of the South*, has written the following description of that crucial moment:

"The hour would rank with any in the history of the world. When the solemn vote was taken and the announcement made that Mississippi had severed her connection with the American Union – had sacrificed all in defense of State sovereignty – a great wave of excitement swept the audience, and grave and dignified men, swayed by a common impulse, joined in the deafening applause." This shout was heard on the outside and was conveyed over the city from street to street, and in almost an instant was signaled throughout the State by the sound of cannon. In the Hall another scene was enacted. The first flag of the Republic of Mississippi was presented to the president of the convention by a group of ladies who were ready to pledge their all in defense of the ordinance. This occasioned much more applause and inspired a spectator to compose and have published on that very day the song, "The Bonnie Blue Flag, That Bears a Single Star."

The last formal step by which the ordinance of secession was incorporated into the body politic of Mississippi was taken on January 15, 1861, when the members of the convention came forward to sign the document as individuals. All but two fixed their signatures to the paper. Mississippi then became a Sovereign Republic.

APPENDIX FIVE
Jefferson Davis' Farewell Address in the United States Senate[1]

I rise, Mr. President [John C. Breckinridge], for the purpose of announcing to the Senate that I have satisfactory evidence that the State of Mississippi, by a solemn ordinance of her people in convention assembled, has declared her separation from the United States. Under these circumstances, of course my functions are terminated here. It has seemed to me proper, however, that I should appear in the Senate to announce that fact to my associates, and I will say but very little more. The occasion does not invite me to go into argument; and my physical condition would not permit me to do so if it were otherwise; and yet it seems to become me to say something on the part of the State I here represent, on an occasion so solemn as this.

---

1. January 21, 1861; *Congressional Globe*, 36th Congress, 2nd Session, p. 487.

It is known to Senators who have served with me here, that I have for many years advocated, as an essential attribute of State sovereignty, the right of a State to secede from the Union. Therefore, if I had not believed there was justifiable cause; if I had thought that Mississippi was acting without sufficient provocation, or without an existing necessity, I should still, under my theory of the Government, because of my allegiance to the State of which I am a citizen, have been bound by her action. I, however, may be permitted to say that I do think she has justifiable cause, and I approve of her act. I conferred with her people before that act was taken, counseled them then that if the state of things which they apprehended should exist when the convention met, they should take the action which they have now adopted.

I hope none who hear me will confound this expression of mine with the advocacy of the right of a State to remain in the Union, and to disregard its constitutional obligations by the nullification of the law. Such is not my theory. Nullification and secession, so often confounded, are indeed antagonistic principles. Nullification is a remedy which it is sought to apply within the Union, and against the agent of the States. It is only to be justified when the agent has violated his constitutional obligation, and a State, assuming to judge for itself, denies the right of the agent thus to act, and appeals to the other States of the Union for a decision; but when the States themselves, and when the people of the States, have so acted as to convince us that they will not regard our constitutional rights, then, and then for the first time, arises the doctrine of secession in its practical application.

A great man who now reposes with his fathers, and who has been often arraigned for a want of fealty to the Union, advocated the doctrine of nullification, because it preserved the Union. It was because of his deep-seated attachment to the Union, his determination to find some remedy for existing ills short of a severance of the ties which bound South Carolina to the other States, that Mr. [John C.] Calhoun advocated the doctrine of nullification, which he proclaimed to be peaceful, to be within the limits of State power, not to disturb the Union, but only to be a means of bringing the agent before the tribunal of the States for their judgment.

Secession belongs to a different class of remedies. It is to be justified upon the basis that the States are sovereign. There was a time when none denied it. I hope the time may come again, when a better comprehension of the theory of our Government, and the inalienable rights of the people of the States, will prevent any one from denying that each State is a sovereign, and thus may reclaim the grants which it has made to any agent whomsoever.

I therefore say I concur in the action of the people of Mississippi, believing it to be necessary and proper, and should have been bound by their action if my belief had been otherwise; and this brings me to the important point which I wish on this last occasion to present to the Senate. It is by this confounding of nullification and secession that the name of a great man, whose ashes now mingle with his mother earth, has been invoked to justify coercion against a seceded State. The phrase "to execute the laws," was an expression which General Jackson applied to the case of a State refusing to obey the laws while yet a member of the Union. That is not the case which is now presented. The laws are to be executed over the United States, and upon the people of the United States. They have no relation to any foreign country. It is a perversion of terms, at least it is a great misapprehension of the case, which cites that expression for application to a State which has withdrawn from the Union. You may make war on a foreign State. If it be the purpose of gentlemen, they may make war against a State which has withdrawn from the Union; but there are no laws of the United States to be executed within the limits of a seceded State. A State finding herself in the condition in which Mississippi has judged she is, in which her safety requires that she should provide for the maintenance of her rights out of the Union, surrenders all the benefits, (and they are known to be many,) deprives herself of the advantages, (they are known to be great,) severs all the ties of affection, (and they are close and enduring,) which have bound her to the Union; and thus divesting herself of every benefit, taking upon herself every burden, she claims to be exempt from any power to execute the laws of the United States within her limits.

I well remember an occasion when Massachusetts was arraigned before the bar of the Senate, and when then the doctrine of coercion was rife and to be applied against her because of the rescue of a fugitive slave in Boston. My opinion then was the same that it is now. Not in a spirit of egotism, but to show that I am not influenced in my opinion because the case is my own, I refer to that time and that occasion as containing the opinion which I then entertained, and on which my present conduct is based. I then said, if Massachusetts, following her through a stated line of conduct, chooses to take the last step which separates her from the Union, it is her right to go, and I will neither vote one dollar nor one man to coerce her back; but will say to her, God speed, in memory of the kind associations which once existed between her and the other States.

It has been a conviction of pressing necessity, it has been a belief that we are to be deprived in the Union of the rights which our fathers bequeathed to us, which has brought Mississippi into her present decision. She has heard proclaimed the theory that all men are created free and equal, and this made the basis of an attack upon her social institutions; and the sacred Declaration of Independence has been invoked to maintain the position of the equality of the races. That Declaration of Independence is to be construed by the circumstances and purposes for which it was made. The communities were declaring their independence; the people of those communities were asserting that no man was born – to use the language of Mr. Jefferson – booted and spurred to ride over the rest of mankind; that men were created equal – meaning the men of the political community; that there was no divine right to rule; that no man inherited the right to govern; that there were no classes by which power and place descended to families, but that all stations were equally within the grasp of each member of the body-politic. These were the great principles they announced; these were the purposes for which they made their declaration; these were the ends to which their enunciation was directed. They have no reference to the slave; else, how happened it that among the items of arraignment made against George III was that he endeavored to do just what the North has been endeavoring of late to do – to stir up insurrection among our slaves? Had the Declaration announced that the negroes were free and equal, how was the Prince to be arraigned for stirring up insurrection among them? And how was this to be enumerated among the high crimes which caused the colonies to sever their connection with the mother country? When our Constitution was formed, the same idea was rendered more palpable, for there we find provision made for that very class of persons as property; they were not put upon the footing of equality with white men--not even upon that of paupers and convicts; but, so far as representation was concerned, were discriminated against as a lower caste, only to be represented in the numerical proportion of three fifths.

Then, Senators, we recur to the compact which binds us together; we recur to the principles upon which our Government was founded; and when you deny them, and when you deny to us the right to withdraw from a Government which thus perverted threatens to be destructive of our rights, we but tread in the path of our fathers when we proclaim our independence, and take the hazard. This is done not in hostility to others, not to injure any section of the country, not even for our own pecuniary benefit; but from the high and solemn motive of defending and protecting the rights we inherited, and which it is our sacred duty to transmit unshorn to our children.

I find in myself, perhaps, a type of the general feeling of my constituents towards yours. I am sure I feel no hostility to you, Senators from the North. I am sure there is not one of you, whatever sharp discussion there may have been between us, to whom I cannot now say, in the presence of my God, I wish you well; and such, I am sure, is the feeling of the people whom I represent towards those whom you represent. I therefore feel that I but express their desire when I say I hope, and they hope, for peaceful relations with you, though we must part. They may be mutually beneficial to us in the future, as they have been in the past, if you so will it. The reverse may bring disaster on every portion of the country; and if you will have it thus, we will invoke the God of our fathers, who delivered them from the power of the lion, to protect us from the ravages of the bear; and thus, putting our trust in God and in our own firm hearts and strong arms, we will vindicate the right as best we may.

In the course of my service here, associated at different times with a great variety of Senators, I see now around me some with whom I have served long; there have been points of collision; but whatever of offense there has been to me, I leave here; I carry with me no hostile remembrance. Whatever offense I have given which has not been redressed, or for which satisfaction has not been demanded, I have, Senators, in this hour of our parting, to offer you my apology for any pain which, in heat of discussion, I have inflicted. I go hence unencumbered of the remembrance of any injury received, and having discharged the duty of making the only reparation in my power for any injury offered.

Mr. President, and Senators, having made the announcement which the occasion seemed to me to require, it only remains to me to bid you a final adieu.

APPENDIX SIX
Biographical Sketch of Alexander H. Handy[1]

The subject of this sketch was born in Somerset County, Maryland, on the 25th of December, 1809. He was well educated, and, having obtained his license as a lawyer, removed to Mississippi in the year 1836. In January, 1837, he was admitted to the bar of the High Court of Errors and Appeals, and entered at once upon a most successful professional career.

In 1853 he was elected to a seat upon the bench of the high Court over Judge William Yerger, who was then upon the bench, but who had rendered himself unpopular with the dominant party in consequence of his opinion in the case of *Johnston vs. The State*, in which he maintained the liability of the State for the payment of the bonds of the Union Bank.

---

1. Extracted from James D. Lynch, *The Bench and Bar of Mississippi* (New York: E.J. Hale and Sons, 1881), pp. 508ff.

Judge Handy held this office until October, 1860, and was then re-elected without opposition.

In 1865 he was again elected a judge of the High Court over George L. Potter, and in January, 1866, was appointed Chief Justice of Mississippi. In November, 1866, he was re-elected without opposition, but resigned the position on the 1st day of October, 1867, by letter to the Governor, in consequence of the court's being placed by the Federal Government in subordination to the military power of the United States.

He then removed to the city of Baltimore and resumed the practice of his profession, but was soon after appointed Professor of Law in the University of Maryland, which position he held until 1871, when he returned to Mississippi and resumed the practice of law at Jackson, and in October, 1877, was admitted to the bar of the Supreme Court of the United States.

Judge Handy has always been a firm believer in the doctrine of States rights, is immovably Southern in his views, and favored secession both as a right and a necessity. He was appointed by the Governor of Mississippi, in December 1860, as a commissioner to the State of Maryland in relation to the political crisis then existing; and failing in his efforts to communicate with the Legislature of that State, in consequence of the refusal of its Governor to convoke that body, Judge Handy addressed himself directly to the people, and in his speech, delivered at at Princes Anne, on the first day of January, 1861, presented the subject of secession – its right and its reason – in a lucid and elaborate manner. He depicted, with the ken of inspiration, the policy and purposes of the party about to take possession of the Federal Government, and showed that the principles announced by the President-elect and the leaders of his party were subversive of all equality in the Union, destructive of the rights of the Southern people, and virtually a revolution of the Government. But, although the people of Maryland were aroused by his presentment of the situation, they could do nothing in view of the action of the State Government.

In 1862 Judge Handy wrote and published a pamphlet entitled "Secession Considered as a Right in the States Composing the Late American Union of States, and as to the Grounds of Justification of the Southern States in Exercising the Right." In this treatise he thoroughly and ably discussed the fundamental principles of the American Government, the conditions upon which it was created, and its interpretation by the authors of the *Federalist.* The work is a profound and instructive constitutional argument, which every lawyer should read who seeks a thorough knowledge of the history, character, and interpretation of the Constitution of the United States.

Judge Handy is a fluent speaker, a polished writer, and an interesting companion. The qualities which so eminently fitted him for a judge designated him for other marks of distinction, and in 1861 the title of LL.D. was tendered him by the faculty and trustees of the University of Mississippi, but his modesty impelled him to decline the honor; and in 1867, on his resignation as a judge of the High Court, he was offered the position of Professor of Law in the same institution, but that was also declined.

As a lawyer Judge Handy is learned and profound, and his legal learning is united to a character of unspotted integrity, and is blended with a purity which eminently fitted him for the bench. As a judge, his uniform urbanity, together with his able and dignified manner of administering justice, excited the admiration of the bar. His decisions are searching and comprehensive, clear and logical in enunciation, and exhaustive in their elucidation of the rights of the parties. His opinions are numerous, and enter largely into the composition of sixteen volumes of the Mississippi Reports, from vol. 26 to vol. 41, inclusive.

They are characterized by an independence of thought and a self-reliance which bespeak the possession of resources rarely acquired, and a fertility of legal genius which only a clear and well-defined sense of right and wrong could inspire, and which only talents of the highest order could develop.

These decisions constitute for his fame a far more splendid and enduring monument than all the pillars and shafts that mechanism could rear, and are records more glorious than all the volumes of praise and adulation that history could produce. Through them his name is inscribed luminously and indelibly upon every title-deed, every tenure, and every relation of the society of Mississippi.

Judge Handy now resides in Canton, Madison County, and is still engaged in the practice of his profession.

www.ingramcontent.com/pod-product-compliance
Lightning Source LLC
Chambersburg PA
CBHW071516040426
42444CB00008B/1665